Creating a
Spiritual
Legacy

Creating a
Spiritual
Legacy

How to Share Your Stories, Values, and Wisdom

DANIEL TAYLOR

BrazosPress

a division of Baker Publishing Group
Grand Rapids, Michigan

Published by Brazos Press
a division of Baker Publishing Group
P.O. Box 6287, Grand Rapids, MI 49516-6287
www.brazospress.com

Printed in the United States of America

Library of Congress Cataloging-in-Publication Data
Taylor, Daniel, 1948–
    Creating a spiritual legacy : how to share your stories, values, and wisdom / Daniel Taylor.
       p.   cm.
    Includes bibliographical references (p.   ).
    ISBN 978-1-58743-275-0 (pbk.)
    1. Autobiography—Religious aspects—Christianity. 2. Storytelling—Religious aspects—Christianity. 3. Christian literature—Authorship. 4. Autobiography—Authorship. I. Title.
    BV4509.5.T393 2011
    248'.5—dc23   2011026254

Scripture quotations labeled NASB are from the New American Standard Bible®, copyright © 1960, 1962, 1963, 1968, 1971, 1972, 1973, 1975, 1977, 1995 by The Lockman Foundation. Used by permission.

Scripture quotations labeled NIV are from the Holy Bible, New International Version®. NIV®. Copyright © 1973, 1978, 1984, 2011 by Biblica, Inc.™ Used by permission of Zondervan. All rights reserved worldwide. www.zondervan.com

11   12   13   14   15   16   17   7   6   5   4   3   2   1

For those who have shared their stories with me
in conversations and classes over the years.
May the blessing of those stories
continue through the generations.

Contents

Acknowledgments

I gratefully acknowledge the insights and fellowship over the years of my colleagues with the Legacy Center: Barry Baines, Doug Baker, Rachael Freed, Bev Lutz, and Mary O'Brien Tyrrell. I also am indebted to our Belfast friends, Rosemary Wilson and Derek and Helen McKelvey, for their wonderful Irish hospitality during the writing of this book. And I wish to acknowledge the legacy of writing and wisdom provided by three masters of the craft: Frederick Buechner, Annie Dillard, and Patricia Hampl.

Introduction

> To lose track of our stories is to be profoundly impoverished not only humanly but also spiritually.
>
> Frederick Buechner

To have a life, you must have a story. In fact, many stories. This is literally true, not merely a metaphor. Your life is not *like* a story; it *is* a story. And if any part of it is to have significance beyond you, this story must be told.

Telling your stories is the central act of a spiritual legacy. It is not a self-indulgence or a passing entertainment. As part of a spiritual legacy, telling your stories is the fulfillment of a responsibility—the responsibility to pass on wisdom. It doesn't matter whether you feel you have wisdom—your stories do.

Every story is unique and, at the same time, every story finds an echo in other stories. Frederick Buechner says, "My story is important not because it is mine, God knows, but because if I tell it anything like right, the chances are you will recognize that in many ways it is also yours." This is one reason why telling your stories is a blessing to others. They see in it something relevant to themselves. Your story provides them resources for living.

Everyone creates an ongoing spiritual legacy each day of life—for good or ill. We are blessed—or harmed—by the examples, virtues, and values of those we share our lives with. Most often our legacy is passed on by actions and by spoken words. But both of these require close contact over a long period of time. And they tend by nature to be transient. Written legacies put stories and insights into forms that stand a much better chance of lasting and of benefiting people at a distance of both time and place.

There is no valid excuse for not creating a more permanent spiritual legacy, least of all a supposed inability to write or tell stories. You could tell a story before you could even talk, and since then you have told them every day of your life. Writing is essentially just putting talk down on paper. If you can't do it (you can), there are others who will do it for you.

Perhaps the surest way to get excited about creating a spiritual legacy is to envision someone you love. He or she needs your stories, needs your insights, needs your wisdom. What greater blessing do you have to offer than the sharing of your life? What more powerful way of sharing a life than telling your stories? Who does not wish to bless those they love? Why not start now?

1

What Is a Spiritual Legacy?

> For we do not, after all, simply have experience; we are entrusted with it. We must do something—make something—with it. A story, we sense, is the only possible habitation for the burden of our witnessing.
>
> Patricia Hampl

A spiritual legacy preserves a life, and life lessons, as a blessing for someone else. The single best way to preserve a life is through story. Because this book is largely about stories, I will begin with one from Marilyn Boe. The Minnesota poet writes in the middle of her life about her own beginnings in a poem titled, "Dad Finds Work During the Great Depression—1934."

> A depression job
> Is what he calls it,
> and it puzzles me
> why he has to show
> me the housing project
> where he fixes what breaks,
> cupboard doors, window panes,
> when tenants pull up their shades,
> unlock their doors
> to him and his toolbox.

He takes me
on the cold streetcar
one Saturday,
the winter I am seven,
far from home,
past boarded up corner stores,
past strange street signs,
a trip of wrong turns,
to a place not Scandinavian,
not South Minneapolis.

He walks past the bums,
says, "Look at those bums!"
and I see threadbare huddles
of slumped coats
that kick the snow,
spit tobacco juice
onto shoveled sidewalks.

I tremble inside my worn snowsuit,
want only to go home,
and he says, "It's all right.
I wanted you to see
we're not really poor,
just out of money
for the time being."

Why does he take me
to a cafe, order sundaes,
a treat as foreign to me
as the Greek he speaks
to the owner, whose
blue, stained-glass window
casts a bruise across
my father's face?

This poem is an example of spiritual legacy. It tells a Depression-era story in present tense from a child's uncomprehending perspective, but with the adult poet not far away. She puts us in the experience with a few revealing visual details—for instance, the bums as "slumped coats/ that kick the snow." The use of dialogue lets us hear her father's voice.

But this is not just a slice of life for its own sake. Her father is trying to teach her something, and the poem is trying to teach us something. Her father's words begin with "It's all right," and that is what he wants his child to feel, not just about what she's seeing, but about their lives in general at this difficult and frightening time. Things are hard, but she and they will be "all right."

He wants her to see the distinction between being "poor"—truly at risk—and simply being "out of money for the time being." He wants her to see that though they are out of money they are still blessed. And he proves it with an extravagant ice cream sundae.

This is a poem—a story—that helps explain to Marilyn Boe the world and her experience in it. Like all master stories, of which we will talk more later, it contains core values that can help her decide how to act in the present and in the future. She can return to this poem later in life when things get tough, and doing so might encourage her to take risks in service to the values of the story.

Notice that the writer doesn't tell us explicitly what the experience means to her. It ends with a question, not an answer. She leaves the reader to come to conclusions, though she provides plenty of clues. This is the way legacy work functions. You can say directly what you think the story means. Or you can just tell it and let it settle into the life of the listener as it may. Either way, it is not hard to see that even a brief story like this could be a blessing to someone she cares about today, a blessing passed on.

This poem shows how spiritual legacy works. Boe's story reminds the writer where she comes from and who she is. It gives her material for thinking about the significance of her life. And it creates something important to say to someone else who will be better for hearing it.

What Is a Spiritual Legacy?

A spiritual legacy is, simply put, the passing of wisdom from one person to another, and such a legacy is the single most important thing you have to give to someone you love.

My dictionary defines *legacy* as money or property left to someone in a will. Not wrong, but far too materialistic and narrow. It offers a second definition of *legacy* as "something" handed down from an ancestor or predecessor or from the past. That definition is more interesting, but it raises the question of what is included in its "something."

A legacy is the radiations of significance from a life—as it is lived and after it is over. It comprises the lingering effects of a person's or institution's or community's actions—for good and bad—in the lives of others. Your legacy is the fragrance of your life that remains when you yourself are not present. It is what your life is or has been good for in a very concrete sense. Everyone creates a legacy as they live, and the ripples of that legacy expand out into eternity.

The question each of us must ask is, What is the "something" that I am passing on to those around me and to those after me? What is the sum effect of my life? Who is better and who is worse because they have come into contact with me? What footprints am I leaving and where do they lead?

Each of these questions will get us thinking about our legacy and how we live. They are as important as any we face in our lives and are one possible starting point for creating a spiritual legacy. But the focus of this book is not on telling you how you ought to live. It is on sharing the life you *have* lived (and *are* living) with others.

The most important legacies are not monetary. The "something" that is handed on in such legacies is spiritual—nonmaterial and more than simply mental. It involves things that last forever, and everyone, without exception, is both the receiver and giver of such legacies.

I will hazard a bookish kind of definition of a spiritual legacy: *A spiritual legacy is the unique complex of values, beliefs, insights, passions, and actions that are embedded in each person's life experiences and can be conveyed to others.* Let me expand a bit on each of these terms.

Unique

Your specific spiritual legacy is as unique as your DNA. No one else has your mix of life experiences or your understandings of what those experiences reveal. You likely share important beliefs and values and passions with others, but your blend of them and how they have worked themselves out in your life are absolutely singular. Martin Luther King Jr. and Malcolm X shared a common commitment to justice, but their lives and their legacies are very different. No two wine lovers or gardeners are the same. Nor any two Jews or Christians.

When we say we share the same beliefs as someone else, we are stating only an approximate truth. I believe in God. Good for me, but what does that mean? What it means is an interweaving of a lifetime of going to church, reading the Bible, listening to preachers and scholars and everyday folks, personal experiences, failures and successes, insights and confusions, reflections and cogitations, actions and failures to act, and on and on. Simply put, my "I believe in God" is not the same as someone else's "I believe in God," even when we are believing in the same God. My "I believe" legacy is not, and could not be, the same as your "I believe" legacy. Therefore, each of us needs to pass on our own legacy.

If our legacies are unique, so is the constellation of people who can benefit from them. There are people in the world whose lives will be better because of your legacy, people who can not receive the same benefit from any other. If your life—and life stories—do not speak to them of goodness and justice and God and perseverance and adventure in the unique way that only yours can, then their lives are diminished. They may pick up some things elsewhere, but not in the way and with the impact that they would from your life. Each of us needs all the positive legacies we can get; if you fail to share yours, someone is going to be one legacy short.

Complex

I use the word *complex* in both the sense of complicated and of many things arranged together. Your life is dense. It is multifaceted, composed of many things, an intricate layering and interweaving of experiences, ideas, feelings—a one-of-a-kind compound of the physical, emotional, and spiritual. In short, your life is not a simple thing and neither is your legacy. Therefore, it cannot be shared with simple maxims or slogans or abstract principles, no matter how true they may be.

Take the Golden Rule, a principle rooted in a God-given truth and found in many cultural traditions: do unto others as you would have them do unto you. This true abstract principle changes few lives, however, until it is conveyed through the details of real-life experiences. The Golden Rule is just another bit of information, but a story from your life that shows the Golden Rule in action has the potential to change someone.

Our lives are complex. Therefore our legacies are complex. And so we need to tell our stories, because stories are the vehicles most suited for embodying meaning-laden complexity.

Values

Human beings are values-soaked creatures. We cannot think, speak, or act for more than a few minutes at a time without revealing a value— a preference for one thing over another or a ranking of priorities. We swim in a constant stream of choices, and every choice we make—trivial or crucial—announces a value. I choose this and not that *because* . . . And in every *because* there lurks a value.

We have at times fooled ourselves into thinking we can be "value free"—as though that would somehow be a good thing (and as though the desire to be so is not itself a value). Freeing ourselves of values—even momentarily—is to free ourselves of our humanity. Rocks and trees are value free, and so are most animals, but valuing—in myriad ways—is part of what makes us human.

And therefore our valuing is a crucial part of our legacy. What is important and not important to us (and these change over time) is a defining part of who we are and a central aspect of our legacy.

People often have problems knowing what to value and why, and in what priority, so any help we can get is important. Ultimately it is not the values we espouse that are telling; it is the values we actually live out in our lives that count. Which is why a spiritual legacy ties values to experience and to action—and thereby to stories, which are the records of our actions.

6

Beliefs

Even people who claim to believe nothing are overflowing with beliefs. Beliefs are convictions about the world that cannot be proved but nonetheless contain some of our most important truths. Where do these convictions come from? Everywhere. Our convictions come from experience, reason, prejudice, emotions, traditions, hunches, desires, and indigestion. If we are values-soaked creatures, we are also belief mongers.

We believe countless things and rarely feel much need to make them logically airtight. But we often back up our important beliefs with a story. Beliefs are not mere whims or arbitrary wishings. Our beliefs grow out of the rich soil of our experience of living. And therefore they are central to our spiritual legacies.

Insights

Insights are life-tested understandings about how things are. Everyone has some. We all learn many things about the details of how life works. We touched a hot stove sometime in our early childhood and since then most of us have had the insight not to do it again.

There are many "hot stoves" in life besides kitchen ones. We learn something about them the hard way and from the cautions of others. There are also many delights in life, and we have insights about those as well. We develop strategies for living, learn to detect the real from the fraudulent, accumulate knowledge about human nature and relationships, discover hidden wonders, and all in all heap up bagfuls of insights about how to navigate life.

Why keep all that to yourself? Even if you don't believe you know the overall meaning of life, there is much that you do know that can be of help to others. These insights are part of your spiritual legacy, and it's your responsibility to share.

Passions

Passions are the fuel that gives energy to values, beliefs, and insights. Without some level of passion—and quiet passion is as useful as the more demonstrative kind—all the good thinking and right values in the world make weak tea. We can all create nice lists of our beliefs and values, but passion turns lists into life, into actions.

If I want to know a person, I want to know what they are passionate about. What gets them out of bed in the morning, motivates them to do the hard thing instead of the easy thing, encourages them to take risks? Passion is a measure of caring, and it is no accident that the source of the word is suffering or pain. I will know your passion when I see what you are willing to suffer for. If it is running, you will be willing to get up very early and run after your legs say stop. If it is justice, you will be willing to speak up when all others are silent. If it is your faith, you will not stop praying until the mountain has moved.

Most people associate passion with the emotions or even with being overtly emotional. But passion is the coming together of all the parts of who we are—the intellect, the heart, the body, and the spirit—to create an energy in service of our valuing. I am passionate about what my mind discovers and my emotions and spirit approve (or vice versa). And I see them as important enough for me to accept pain as the price for making them an actual part of my world. Some people suffer to make fortunes, some to run fast, some to bless their children, some to build God's kingdom.

Tell me what you will suffer for, and I will consider whether it is something I should be willing to suffer for—to be passionate about—as well. It is part of your legacy, and it could become part of mine.

Actions

A unique complex of values, beliefs, insights, and passions that did not result in actions would be a much-diminished legacy. We have a lot of folk sayings for such a situation, including "All talk and no action" and, in Texas (where I spent part of my childhood), "All hat and no oil." The unpleasant single-word description is *hypocrite*.

And this gap between convictions and actions is the sadly emaciated legacy of many people who think it enough to merely *believe* the right things, whether in politics, social values, or religion. Your legacy is much more embodied in your actions than in your disembodied beliefs

8

and values. The goal, of course, is that your actions grow out of and confirm your beliefs and values.

Actions not only lend credibility to our beliefs and values, but they also speak to the possibility for change. If my actions change, perhaps because experience deepens or modifies my values, then I change. My life is different; it is not the life I once lived, and I, to that extent, am not the person I once was. That fact changes my impact on the world around me. It also changes my legacy and can, thereby, change others.

Embedded

The last part of my definition of spiritual legacy reads, "that are embedded in each person's life experiences and can be conveyed to others." A spiritual legacy cannot be detached from the messy particulars of the life that produces it. It is entangled, concrete, specific, and rooted in time and place. Your entire life is your legacy, which is why we need to pay attention to how we live.

It is also why stories are the single best way to convey a legacy. Stories too are rooted and particular and messy. That is because stories are modeled after the way our brains process the endless flow of data that threatens to overwhelm them. The brain is constantly looking for a narrative thread in that data, and the stories we tell mirror that quest.

If you want to share your legacy—and you should want to—you must tell us your stories, because your legacy is embedded in them. Tell the stories of failure and pain as well as those of success and gladness. Because such is the stuff of our own stories, and we need to hear of both.

Life Experiences

Everything that happens to you, whether you choose it or it chooses you, is included in your life experiences. These are the raw materials that compost into your legacy. They may include experiences that were originally toxic but have been transformed over time, through the action of grace, into the rich soil of your legacy.

A black African character in the play *Master Harold and the Boys* by Athol Fugard, after a promising afternoon ends bitterly with a white boy spitting in his face, says to the boy that it would be a shame if "nothing has been learnt in here this afternoon," because "there was a hell of a lot of teaching going on." The same can be said for our lives, bitter or sweet. In each of our lives there is a whole lot of teaching going on, and we have the opportunity to share what we have learned with those we care about.

Conveyed

In one sense we cannot help but pass on a legacy. We influence each other's lives, for better or worse, as the sun influences everything on which it shines. If there are six billion people now on the earth, there are six billion unique legacies being created, each of which actively shapes the life of dozens (or maybe millions) of other people. Given the viral and exponential nature of human relationships, the daily legacies of even the most secluded of us ripple through many lives, around the world and through the generations.

Even though legacy leaving is inescapable, we can purpose to make our legacy more explicit and more positive than it might otherwise be. My life is a legacy no matter what, but I can make it more powerful and more healing by consciously choosing to share it with others. I can tell the stories and express the insights that otherwise might die with me. A story not repeated is a story lost. And with the loss of any story, we lose the unique complex of values, beliefs, insights, passions, and actions that inhere within it. And everyone is the worse.

To Others

Sharing a spiritual legacy has many benefits for the one doing the sharing, as we will see. But spiritual legacies exist, ultimately, for the benefit of people we love. This, to me, is what distinguishes spiritual legacy work from autobiography and memoir, even when the latter are focused on matters of the spirit. Autobiography and memoir tend to be inward focused, reporting on or probing a life to see what it yields. They usually are written with no particular reader in mind, addressed to anyone who is interested.

Spiritual legacy work is also inward focused, of course. But it has within it a conscious outward movement toward others, usually toward an identifiable and well-known other. In this work one never loses sight of the goal of providing spiritual nurture and life guidance to someone else—even if it is, for example, to a future great-grandchild you will never know, but who needs to know something of you and your life.

So there is in spiritual legacy work a simultaneous looking inward and looking outward. You investigate your life not because you are fascinated with yourself or self-absorbed but because you believe that within the details of your life is nurture for another life. In many cases, you are simply passing on the blessings that have been passed on by others to you.

A Shorter Definition

I think the preceding definition of spiritual legacy is accurate and helpful, but it is also too long and abstract to keep in one's head. Here is a shorter one: *a spiritual legacy is an offering of wisdom from one life to another.*

It is an offering because it is voluntarily given and voluntarily received. There is no coercion or insistence or hectoring in a true spiritual legacy. The legacy is there to be received, reflected and acted on—or not. It is also an offering because it is given not to the universe in general but specifically to someone who is valued, as in an offering to God.

The single word that best sums up the rich offering of a spiritual legacy is *wisdom*. Wisdom is not to be confused with intelligence or education. There are many intelligent and educated fools, and many of the simple and sparsely educated are wise.

Wisdom is practical knowledge about the nature of the world and how to live well in it. It is a combination of right priorities and right actions: knowing the relative significance of things and acting accordingly. The wise person knows, for instance, that loving relationships are more important than money, and makes choices accordingly. Everyone acknowledges that truth abstractly, but the wise actually shape their lives around it.

Roger Schank, in a book exploring the relationship between story and intelligence, links wisdom with storytelling: "Wisdom is often ascribed to those who can tell just the right story at the right moment." Wisdom is the ability to call to mind the story most fitting and most helpful in a given situation.

This is not to say that only the wisest among us have something to offer to another. Everyone has learned something from his or her life—even if it is only what not to do. Each of us has a portion of wisdom, often hard and painfully won, that can lighten the way of another. And each of us has the responsibility to share it.

A Place for What Cannot Be Buried or Sold

Buckminster Fuller used to ask audiences to imagine that he was holding in his hand a rope. He tied a loose knot in that imaginary rope and asked them to visualize the knot moving along as it was passed down the rope. He would ask the audience what the knot consisted of, given that the section of the physical rope that made it visible was changing from moment to moment. He then suggested that the knot did not consist of rope but was instead the patterned configuration that the rope made visible.

Fuller suggested that the same is true for us. Every atom that makes us up is replaced by a different atom within a handful of years. Who is the *me* that persists over the years? It is not the atoms that form my body, because they change. It is a configuration, a pattern, and I would propose that it is essentially spiritual. Your body makes visible that spiritual signature that is uniquely you. And your legacy is to leave something of that spiritual signature in the life of another person.

We have a number of customs and rituals for dealing with the time when we will no longer be physically present in the world. We write living wills to indicate how we want our bodies treated at the end of our lives. We write financial wills to indicate how our property should be distributed. But what about those aspects of who we are that cannot be buried in the ground or sold at a garage sale? What about our values and insights, our character and personality, our life experiences, and how we made sense of it all? What about our hard-earned wisdom—or best shots at it? What customs or rituals do we have for those defining characteristics of who we are?

The gerontologist James Birren observes, "We have large cemeteries to collect our bones, but what do we have to collect our stories?" Other people can bury you. Other people can divide up your property. But only you can tell your stories.

These questions apply as much to the young and middle-aged as to the old. How can I give shape to what I am learning from life even as I am living and learning from it? How can I snatch something from the rushing flood of living and hold it up for contemplation and preservation? Is there any sense to be made of all this as it is happening, and if so, how can I share it? Who can help me? Whom can I help?

There are many answers to all these questions. And the thing those answers have in common is story.

The Legacy-Preserving Nature of Stories

Stories are the single best way to capture and make sense of our experience. When we need to explain or preserve something that has happened—or is happening or will happen—we make a story. The story may be the "Once upon a time" of fantasy, or the "Early in the morning on June 6, 1944" of history, or the "Then it was noticed that mold in a petri dish stopped the growth of bacteria" of science, or the "In the beginning God" of religious faith. Whenever we need insight (or comfort or nurture or simply entertainment), it is story we most often turn to.

There are reasons why story is so central to our lives (which I explore more fully in my book *Tell Me a Story*). Here, briefly stated, are a few.

We Live in Stories

We tell stories because our lives present themselves to us in story form: setting, characters, plot. Life is not like a novel. Novels are like life, and that is why we read them. We tell and listen to stories obsessively because nothing else so compelling organizes the disparate bits of our lives.

13

We don't simply hear stories, we live within them. Everything I believe and think and do can be linked to a story that I have consciously or unconsciously embraced. My mental and emotional life, my political and social convictions, my religious faith, my boyhood love of the Dodgers, can all be tied to stories. I grew up, for instance, with the stories of the Bible echoing through my head and heart. I didn't just *hear* them, or simply *believe* them; I processed reality *through* them. David taking on Goliath told me what I had to do when the playground bully was picking on a little kid.

We are born into stories that have been going on long before we arrived. Those stories receive us, shape us, nurture us, and explain the world to us. We inhale and exhale stories throughout our lives. They offer an answer for life's big questions. They tell us what is right and what is wrong, who to believe and who not to believe. Stories tell us what to do, and they admonish us when we fail to do it.

Stories not only shape our morality, but they also tell us how to vote, what makes a good job good, whom to marry, and what a successful life is. Because they do all this, and much more, our store of stories is never full enough. We are always better for another healthy story, another account of some aspect of the human experience. A fresh story, especially from someone who wishes us well, replenishes our resources for living. Tell me your story and you add to my story.

Stories are the natural vehicle for making sense of the world and therefore are the natural means for sharing a legacy.

Stories Are Holistic

Stories engage us from the tops of our heads to the bottoms of our feet and all points in between. Stories transcend our categories. They reject any too-neat division of human beings into intellect, emotion, body, and soul. Stories seize us in our entirety, making equal and integrated appeal to all that we are. Stories make us think, make us feel and imagine, enlarge or diminish our souls, and play a tune on our bodies. When I first saw the wicked witch in *The Wizard of Oz* (watched largely through fingers over my eyes), my heart thumped, my emotions surged, and my reason counseled Dorothy to stick tight in those ruby slippers.

14

All of me was engaged, all of me was frightened, and all of me wanted to see what happened next.

Stories are holistic and, therefore, so are our legacies.

Stories Make Connections

Human beings have an innate and irrepressible need for some level of order and meaning in their lives. Stories, better than anything else, serve that need. It is the essence of plot to connect one event to another in a meaningful way—one thing happens *because* another thing happened. Story insists on cause and effect, even in the midst of seeming randomness.

The brain is wired to look for a narrative thread in all the data that floods it. Human consciousness depends on the brain's ability to discern a plot in the mass of data sent to it by the senses—or to create a plot. At a higher level, we are constantly looking for a meaningful plot to our lives, for connections between things. Our fear that life is random and meaningless is stronger than the fear of want or violence.

Engaging other people's stories helps us make a story of our own to live in. It is similar to providing a painter with a model or landscape to look at while painting. Seeing something helps me paint it. A story legacy adds to our ability to sort out our lives. It can model connectedness and encourage me to find or make similar connections within my own story.

This increased sense of connectedness happens both for the one who tells the stories and the one who receives them, helping them both better understand the meaning of their own lives. When my father told me, in story form, that he had married my mother against his better judgment, I understood something more about them and something more about the home in which I was growing up.

We want life to make some kind of sense, and stories give us hope that it does. Story legacies allow us to share what we've learned.

Stories Create Communities

Human beings are innately social creatures, and stories are the single most powerful glue that binds us together. One definition of a community is people who share common stories. People know who they are and who they belong to by the stories that they tell together.

A sense of togetherness rooted in shared stories is certainly evident in families: stories are thicker than blood. It is less important that a child shares the genes of the rest of a family than that he or she knows and participates in the stories of the family. We did these things together; we tell these stories about our shared experiences; we laugh and cry and argue about the same storied past—therefore we are a family. ("Remember when Uncle Louie threw the Christmas turkey out the window?") We are characters in each other's stories.

The same is true for ethnic groups and nations. I have more than once attended swearing-in ceremonies in which immigrants became United States citizens. Every color, creed, body shape, personality, and culture is represented. What they swear to, and what the speeches and storytelling and songs and pledges reinforce, is that now they are joining a new story, one in which they are characters with roles to play and a common good to work toward.

And of course commitment to shared stories is what holds religions together. When I attended a church service in Seoul and heard one of the gospel stories preached in Korean, I knew I was in a community of fellow believers. And when they sang the same songs I did as a child in Texas in the 1950s, I knew that we also shared some particular ancestors. We didn't look alike, or have the same culture, nor were we related by blood or politics, but we shared core, life-defining stories in common, and so we recognized each other, though we had never met.

Story-based community works at the smallest level. When people share their stories with us, they invite us into a relationship with them. Every telling of a story creates a community of at least two. It works even if one of us is dead, and even if we have never met. When I read the book of Acts, I am one of the apostles. Luke has invited me into that community. When I tell stories from my own life, I send them out as a similar invitation to whomever hears them. "Here are my stories; I hope they help you with yours. We are in this together."

Stories can do this. They can leap over the many gaps between one life and another and tell us what we have in common. What better vehicle for a legacy?

Stories Encourage Us to Act

A healthy human being is a verb, not merely a noun. To fully realize what we were created to be, we must act, not simply exist. Stories encourage action by placing us as characters within a story. The essence of being a character is making choices—good or bad, with wonderful or disastrous consequences—or more often something in between. (Think Moses, Antigone, Socrates, Peter, Thomas More, Bonhoeffer, Frodo.) A novel with passive characters is a lousy novel, and a life with a passive central character is a lousy life.

If you are exactly the same person after hearing a story as before, the story has not done you any good. It has been literally meaningless, a killing of time. Stories encourage us to see ourselves as characters in our own story. And the essence of being a character is making choices. This is why stories are inevitably value-laden. Every choice implies an ought—I choose this and not that *because* . . . We cannot explain the *because* without invoking a value of some kind, whether profound or merely pragmatic.

It is the necessity of choosing that defines both a character and the quality we call *character*. Virtues, the qualities that make up our character, are values in action—that is, values brought to life by the choices and actions of a character. When I read the story of Sojourner Truth or Nelson Mandela and see the choices they made under pressure, something tells me I should be a bit more like them. That something is the wisdom conveyed by the story. If I take their stories to heart and act on them, my own story is better than it otherwise would have been. Stories shape our character and therefore shape the choices we make in our everyday lives. I become who I am by modeling the actions of the characters in the stories that I embrace.

A spiritual legacy is an implicit call to action to the one who receives it. It doesn't offer itself as mere entertainment, something to kill the time. It offers itself as help for living, something to redeem the time. It doesn't claim to answer every question or solve every riddle, but it says, "Here's what happened to me. Here's what I think I've learned from it. I hope this is helpful to you." And it will be helpful if we use such legacies as we make our own choices as characters within our own story, which we can then share with others.

Stories Tell Us What to Do

Stories are not content with just any action. A good story is directive. It is not preachy or lecturing or bullying or necessarily explicit in its directing, but it rejects the idea that all choices are equally valid. Because story believes in cause and effect, it knows that some causes have disastrous effects and that in a fallen world not even a good choice guarantees that all will be well.

Stories usually do not tell us *precisely* what to do, but they point directions. Tell a child a story about failure and you will not prevent the child from ever failing. But you will help the child understand that everyone fails at some point or another, a comfort to a child who perhaps thinks failure is unique to him- or herself. And your story may teach the child something about how to *respond* to failure that will help them when they do fail.

These are some of the reasons why story legacies are important. There are many others, some of which you will discover as you tell your stories. And there are other ways to pass on a spiritual legacy without stories, even without words, that we will also explore.

Not Just for the Gray-Haired

If you think you're too young for this "looking-back-at-my-life" stuff, then you haven't understood what I'm saying. Forget the "back" part and just consider "looking at my life." Jesus was in the temple discoursing with the wise when he was twelve. You and I aren't Jesus, but we have minds, hearts, bodies, and spirits—and a growing pile of life experiences to make sense of. And someone you care about will benefit from your efforts, even if the benefit comes many years from now. (You may even be writing, in part, for your future self!) Most of the people who meant a lot to you and have already passed away were once your age. Would you not value knowing how they thought, a story from when they were a teenager or in their twenties or thirties? You should provide such a blessing to somebody else.

Consider Rachael's story.

I got to know Rachael when she joined a group of students that I took to Cuba to study writing and Hemingway and to get away from a Minnesota January.

I have in front of me three photographs from Rachael's wedding day, not too long after that trip to Cuba. The first photograph is of a serious Rachael on her solemn day—solemn in the medieval sense of the word, meaning (as Thomas Howard reminds us) both joyous and weighted with significance (as in a solemn occasion, such as a wedding or a coronation). In the second photograph Rachael is laughing extravagantly, as she often did. She is standing in her long wedding dress, looking down at her new husband, taking pleasure in him and in the occasion.

I believe that Rachael could laugh this way not only because it was part of her personality, but also because she had a story to live by. She was not just a believer, someone who believed certain assertions about life, she was someone deeply and passionately caught up in God's story for the world and her part in it.

Rachael was incurably curious: she was smart, she wrote excellent poems, she did everything she could to squeeze all the juice out of life. When she was a child, a teacher asked her to identify something she was afraid of. She wrote, "I am afraid of having a mediocre life."

And she lived so as to defeat mediocrity: she went twice to Spain, and with us to Cuba; she was game for any adventure—physical or intellectual or spiritual; she was devoted to friendship and to literature; and she soaked herself in Bible study and prayer with a kind of discipline rare among Christians of any age. Rachael actually thought it was possible to be godly—that is, to live her life as though God were real—and she thought she should try.

When she went to Spain the second time, she told her best friend that they could not email each other, only write letters, because letters meant more. Her biggest fear in life was missing out—missing out on anything that life had to offer—especially missing something because she was afraid to fail or was passive or indifferent.

19

She had all the energy and intensity and idealism of youth—and yet, somehow, it didn't seem naive. You got the feeling she had some wisdom about ultimate things that you did not, and that it was your skepticism that was naive.

From Spain she wrote the following to her friend:

Remember: as far as I understand it in this world, it's not good versus evil, love versus hate. No! It's love versus nothing. So fight against nothing, the mass nada. Love against the lack of love.

Hope. Hope because there just might be a tomorrow. Hope brings into existence . . . that which we want to be. Don't accept the pessimism. Recognize the problem. Hope in God—"for I shall yet praise him."

And Rachael knew about being a character in God's story and about having her own actions shaped by Christ's actions. When we went to Cuba, I told the students to bring small gifts—practical things like aspirin or writing pens or even bars of soap. When we were in Santiago, Rachael was approached by a little boy, around four or five, who asked her in Spanish for money. He said he wanted to buy some candy.

Because she had committed herself to learning Spanish (German and Japanese were next), she was ready for the question. She got down on her knees, so she could look the little *niño* in the eye, and said to him in his own language, "I don't have any money, but how would you like this?" And she pulled from her bag a shiny, new baseball.

His eyes got huge. Living in a country where poor kids play baseball with a tree limb for a bat and wadded up tape for a ball, he might never have used a real baseball. He was so stunned by his good fortune that he could not move. Rachael's was a simple act of kindness—one quality of a healthy life story.

I have felt Rachael's kindness myself. Before we went to Cuba, she was in one of my classes. If you remember anything about school, you perhaps remember that teachers sometimes get the feeling that no one is listening, no one is taking this stuff seriously—thinking that maybe, just maybe, they should have taken that job in advertising after all. Sometimes it shows on our faces, or in little cynical comments we make in self-defense. Perhaps Rachael saw or heard that from me one day.

20

Whatever the reason, I found a handwritten poem on my door—with no name on it. It ended something like this:

> Speak on, oh grey beard,
> Some of us are listening.

Rachael sent me this poem anonymously, as an encouragement. It was an act of kindness.

How do I know it was from her? I found out at a memorial reading we had for Rachael at our university. Her best friend, Amber, had helped her write it. For you see, the photographs from Rachael's wedding served double duty. They were also used on her funeral program a few months later.

Rachael had been to a bridal shower for her soon-to-be sister-in-law. Rachael told her how thrilled she was to finally have a sister. And a few minutes after she left the shower, her car was hit by a truck and she was sent suddenly into eternity. That third photograph from her wedding shows her getting into a car and leaving us—and so she did.

It is good that Rachael had a story to live by, because, unbeknownst to us (but perhaps not to her), it was chosen that her life was to be short. If Rachael had waited to find a story to live by, waited to have all her questions answered, she would never have found one at all.

Life is too precarious to live even a single day without a story.

In another of her letters from Spain, Rachael quotes from St. Teresa of Avila, "a saint to learn from in the short course of my life." She gives Teresa's words in Spanish and then translates them herself: "You must always remember that you don't have more than one soul, you have but to die one death, you have nothing more than one brief life, there is nothing more but one glory, and it is eternal, and so give your hands to many things."

Rachael gave her hands to many things, and so should we. She committed herself to a story, one that told her how to live, and she lived fully, if not long, just as her Creator intended.

That's my story about Rachael, one among many that could be told. Rachael's legacy includes me, her teacher. Now I am her student. She has taught me things I need to know, wise things, things of the gospel and shalom. Much of what I learned from her, however, depended on her preserving her reflections in words. She was one of many students on the trip, and our lives afterward only intersected here and there. I did not know her well before she died. But then I found she had written me the poem, and her friend shared parts of the letters she had written from Spain, and I listened as others testified to what they had learned from her life.

If Rachael had waited to live longer before she reflected on her life, she would have waited too long. Her legacy would be diminished. We would never have read her poems. We would never have learned what she learned from St. Teresa. We would know less of her and we would be diminished ourselves.

This is what legacy work is—one person sharing his or her life with another. Passing on wisdom. But it is important to add that the significance of her legacy work does not depend on her having died. Her legacy would have been just as important had Rachael lived to be a great-grandmother. Others would have been blessed by what she wrote when she was young.

This is work we should do at every age, because it gives importance to our living before it lends significance to our dying.

2

The Spiritual Will

Wisdom comes softly, unexpectedly, through the everyday circumstances of living. It just happens.

Arthur Lynip

All spiritual legacy work starts with reflection. You must think about your life, not just exist in it. You must, at least occasionally, chew on it, walk around it, poke at it, analyze it, make assessments of it. When you buy a used car, you look under the hood and kick the tires; when you consider your legacy, you do the same.

This reflection goes both forward and backward. Forward-looking questions include, what do I want my legacy to be? and, who do I want my legacy to bless? The answers to such questions about the future can deeply influence present actions. If I want my legacy to be *that*, then I will have to do *this* in the present. Do I, for instance, want generosity or service to be part of my legacy? Then I will necessarily need to do the deeds in the present that create such a legacy. (This is an added value of legacy work: it encourages us to live more concretely the values we espouse.)

Legacy work requires us to look back as well—back over our experiences, our relationships, our actions. It prompts us to ask big questions:

What have I done in and with my life?

What have I learned?

What do I value?

What is most important in life and how has my answer to that changed over time?

When have I been happiest or felt my life had the most meaning?

What have I learned the hard way that I want someone else to learn more easily?

What can I pass on to others that will make their lives better or easier or deeper?

What stories capture all this?

(See appendix A, "Spiritual Legacy Questions," for more questions.)

If the first step is to reflect on your life and identify some of what you wish to pass on to others, the second step is to decide on a method of preservation. You *have* a legacy that needs to be preserved. There is no question about that. But *how* are you going to preserve it? How is the wisdom that grows out of your life going to be passed on to someone you care about?

As we have seen, we all pass on something of our legacy—for good or ill—directly into the lives of others with whom we come into contact. We leave an imprint on every person whose life intersects our own. So our lives leave a legacy whether we ever give it a thought or not.

But we can have more than random or accidental legacies. We can purpose to reflect thoughtfully on what our legacy is, what we want it to be, how it can be preserved, and how we can use it to enrich the lives of people we care about. There are many methods, and most of them are rooted in stories.

24

The Spiritual Will

One of the oldest methods of passing on a spiritual legacy is the ethical will, sometimes called the spiritual-ethical will. For simplicity's sake, I will most often call it a spiritual will, because it primarily pertains to things of the spirit. This approach requires no great writing skills and no prolonged effort. But it does require serious reflection and life assessment. It is a basic and yet potentially profound approach to leaving a spiritual legacy to those you love.

We use a "material will," on the one hand, to disperse the money and material things we have acquired, usually in the latter part of life. A spiritual will, on the other hand, is used for what Barry Baines calls "the disposition of 'moral' assets," and is equally valuable at all stages of life. It was especially useful in the past for women, who often were denied ownership of property and therefore had only wisdom and spiritual insights to pass on, as Rachael Freed has pointed out. Baines observes, "Legal wills bequeath *valuables*, while ethical wills bequeath *values*" (his emphasis).

A Definition

Here is a definition: *A spiritual will is a personal statement (often quite brief) about what one has learned from one's life—created for the benefit of others*. It combines wisdom and blessing.

A spiritual will focuses on what is important, on life lessons, on insights reaped from experience. It tends to be succinct, offering the lessons learned from life more often than the complete stories out of which those lessons grow. It is an *epitome* of a life with an emphasis on values, a distillation in a few pages—or paragraphs—of serious thinking about a lifetime of living. And it is best offered as a blessing to someone you care about.

The term "ethical will" comes from the Jewish tradition. In that tradition, as a man approached the point of death he would gather his family around and make final declarations. Some had economic implications, but others, more importantly, passed on his blessing and wisdom to those he loved.

The oldest record of an ethical will is Jacob's pronouncements on his sons—more curses, alas, than blessings—in Genesis 49. In this instance, Jacob speaks of the future of his sons based on their past actions. He speaks to them in terms of the law of sowing and reaping, emphasizing that actions have consequences. As they have sown in life, Jacob suggests, so they will reap. ("He blessed them, every one with the blessing appropriate to him" Gen. 49:28 NASB.) Jacob's is a harsh wisdom, with only Joseph receiving an unreserved blessing, and shows a less forgiving spirit than is generally advisable for a spiritual will. Painfully, it does not include his daughters.

Jesus gives something of an ethical will at the Last Supper. Knowing he is about to die, he presents important final teachings to the disciples, reviewing what they had learned before, giving the "new commandment" to "love one another," and promising they will understand more after his death when the Holy Spirit comes. He adds, "These things I did not say to you at the beginning, because I was with you" (John 16:4 NASB). We say things in a spiritual-ethical will that speak to the past, present, and future, knowing that we will not always be here to say the thing that needs to be said. It is precisely because we will not always be here that such a statement is necessary.

This Jewish tradition of preserving final words has persisted down to the present, modified and expanded over time to include women, and importantly for our purposes, broadened to be used at any time in life. A spiritual will is as appropriate at twenty as at seventy. It represents a statement, at a particular point in time, of one's values, vision of the world, core convictions, guiding principles, or personal observations. It is what you have learned to date, subject to later modification, amplification, or even repudiation. It doesn't claim to be the final word on anything, but it is *a* word, a stake in the ground that expresses, for someone else's benefit or pleasure, what you believe is important.

Though it has religious roots, the spiritual will today can as easily be secular as religious. Its content and form is entirely up to the person creating it. That person, in fact, does not even have to be aware of the spiritual-ethical will tradition. Whenever one is trying to succinctly express core values and insights, he or she is doing legacy work in the spirit of the ethical will.

The Russian novelist Aleksandr Solzhenitsyn, for instance, in a passage from his historical and autobiographical chronicle of his time in the Stalinist concentration camps, *The Gulag Archipelago*, is participating in a long tradition when he offers this condensed assessment of life's priorities:

> What about the main thing in life, all its riddles? If you want, I'll spell it out for you right now. Do not pursue what is illusory—property and position—all that is gained at the expense of your nerves decade after decade, and is confiscated in one fell night. Live with a steady superiority over life—don't be afraid of misfortune, and do not yearn after happiness; . . . whom should you envy? And why? Our envy of others devours us most of all. Rub your eyes and purify your heart—and prize above all else in the world those who love you and wish you well. Do not hurt them or scold them, and never part from any of them in anger; after all, you simply do not know: it might be the last act before your arrest, and that will be how you are imprinted on their memory.

This, like all spiritual wills, is a concise statement of core values. It sums up much that Solzhenitsyn learned about life, as refined by the fires of suffering. Do not pursue illusions, especially those tied to possessions and power and prestige. Do not live in fear. Do not worship comfort or be afraid to suffer. Do not envy others. Every material thing you put your faith in can be torn from you in an instant.

These are the "thou shall nots" of Solzhenitsyn's declaration. Then comes the positive command: prize those who love you. Value them above all earthly things. Each time you are with them, treat them with the same tenderness as you would were you never to see them again—for such might in fact be the case.

These words are part of Solzhenitsyn's spiritual legacy, available to anyone who reads them. I often think of them when my own children walk out the door—and so try to part from them with a blessing. Imagine finding such words in a letter written by someone you care deeply about whose life is over (as Solzhenitsyn's now is). Think how much it would mean to you, and how life-shaping it might be, to hear such wisdom from someone you respect and love—living or dead. Such is the potential power of a spiritual will.

If you are looking for something a little less weighty than admonitions from a Russian novelist, consider the more folksy words of Lee Pitts in *People Who Live at the End of Dirt Roads*. In a piece directed to the young, he offers a list of "hopes" for them, most of them showing a preference for old-fashioned ways of raising kids. He hopes they learn something about hand-me-down clothes, and earning things instead of being given them, and skinning their knee from trying something risky, and similar life experiences. In each case, he ties an abstract value to a concrete manifestation of that value. For example, "If you want a slingshot, I hope that your mother doesn't just fork over the money and that your father is around to teach you how to make one."

When I first read this bit of wisdom, I thought of my own grandfather and the Ohio River. Sam Hicks was a no-nonsense railroad man who lived in Maysville, Kentucky, on the river. My family lived with him for one summer when there wasn't enough money to live on our own, and I remember laboring in his woodshop, under his critical eye, to build a toy boat worthy of the mighty Ohio River. I spent hours sawing, sanding, and nailing. It was to be a paddleboat of sorts, rubber-band propelled, and I had visions of it going on its own power at least across the river, if not all the way to New Orleans.

As it turned out, despite multiple rubber bands and three separate wood-chip paddles, once in the river it didn't travel even three feet—and not in a straight line at that. A great failure. But I remember that boat, the hopes that went into it and my grandfather's role, in a way I never would have remembered a boat that was given to me ready-made. So when Pitts hopes for a homemade slingshot created with Dad (we made those too), I know what he's talking about and I recognize the wisdom that he is offering.

It works for abstractions too. "I hope," he says, "you get a black eye fighting for something you believe in." Believing in something is abstract and a bit bloodless. Fighting for something is tangible, sensory, and gets the blood moving. Being for justice is a value; fighting for justice is a virtue—a value in action. When we write a spiritual will, we should look for the words that make our values sound as though they are connected to the real world by how we live.

These "spiritual wills" of Solzhenitsyn and Pitts share some things in common. They are written for the benefit of others. They are both full of insight and wisdom. They are both rooted in real life and are simultaneously timeless, expressing truths that will never cease to be true. And both are full of love. Each is a spiritual legacy—a blessing—that benefits those to whom it is directed more than any amount of money or property.

And it is something that anyone, including you, can do—in a few minutes if necessary.

The Benefits of Spiritual Wills

Creating a spiritual will benefits both creator and receiver, most fundamentally by affirming a particular life—and life in general. (See Baines in the "Resources" for an extended list of benefits.) In reflecting on and expressing your core values, you come to better understand who you are and the meaning of your own life. By tying those values to specific experiences, you see more clearly their significance. Your own life comes to seem less random, less ordinary, less superficial. A spiritual will allows you to preserve what should not be lost. It contributes to a collective family and community-wide memory—a memory of people, experiences, and commitments whose value is beyond calculation.

A spiritual will also gives you a chance to say at an appropriate distance what is difficult, sometimes impossible, to say face-to-face. You can express carefully in writing things that might come out all wrong if spoken. You can ask forgiveness and express gratitude. You can be honest about disappointments and failures while still emphasizing blessings and joys.

Not least, a spiritual will allows you to come to terms with your own finitude—whether written near the end of a life or in its prime. We are all going to die, and creating a spiritual will frees one to accept that reality by offering evidence of the purpose for which one has lived. It does not require that you entirely understand or are happy with your life to that point, only that you have learned some things that might help someone else.

A spiritual will says, "Here's what I think I've learned," not, "Here is the final truth for the ages." It is best written in a spirit of confident humility—confident that one has some insight, humility because of much one still doesn't know and because life is difficult. Spiritual wills are not a place to pontificate or upbraid or get even. Author Jack Reimer warns against issuing "a grudge from the grave." They are a place to encourage, affirm, and guide. They are a place, in short, to pass on wisdom.

Consider, for example, the following from a much-loved college professor of mine, who is near the end of a very long and blessed life. Approaching ninety-six years of age, and no longer able to see well, he dictates letters to his daughter-in-law Karen, wanting to respond to the many greetings he still receives from former students "before I reach my final address."

> Dear friends,
> I have a raft of letters on my desk, each of immense significance to me; but I can't see or even read my own writing. I want to be able to respond to each of you personally. My will is wrapped up in a variety of intentions. Just the other evening, while dozing, the proposition came to me that I should write just one letter to everyone. I shall try.
> First of all, I love you dearly. You are my past and also my present and together we trust the Lord for the future. For you are the people with whom I hope to spend eternity. Here is the contour of my present. I am like others who have grown into senility with capacities dropped away one by one. My faculties are cut back. There sit my best friends' letters of inquiry and testimony and I can't respond to them each personally. Please accept my confession and apology.
> I am with you day after day and night after night.
> Your beloved Arthur

This is very brief and, in one sense, doesn't say a great deal. That is, it doesn't address in any detail his life, or life in general. But, at the same time, it says everything. It testifies to his life and core convictions—his valuing of friendship, his hopes for eternity, his desire to bless those he loves but is separated from, and his general openheartedness.

In another letter, he writes the following:

> God has manifested Himself through every aspect of nature and existence and weather. The Creator does reveal Himself. People are inclined to look for God in nature and its manifestations—a glacier, a cavern, an animal or other physical demonstrations of His essence. God demonstrates who He is to every living being. In every event—big, small, or indifferent—He is there as an audience of one.

Here he is openly teaching, as he did for so many years. He is passing on wisdom.

Everything he writes speaks to his desire to end his life well. As his daughter-in-law says, "He chooses Joy even when he remembers conversations and situations in life that he knows he handled poorly. He is appreciative of our investments in him and wants to live out his days in a flow of Grace. It is both a convicting and enriching drama to be drawn right into the middle of." And by passing on what he still can to those who have known and loved him, he draws us into the flow of grace as well.

In writing these letters, Dr. Lynip is not consciously writing a "spiritual will," but he is quite consciously desiring to be a blessing to those he cares about. Spiritual wills often take the form of letters, and that might be the form in which you wish to write one yourself.

Receiving a Spiritual Will

If creating a spiritual will is life affirming, receiving one can be life changing. It can provide insight, direction, encouragement, comfort, reconciliation, a sense of belonging and community, and, not least, simple pleasure. If someone cares enough to share his or her life with you in the intimacy of a spiritual will, you cannot help but feel more bonded to that person, even if a relationship had previously been strained.

How do we learn how to live well? One way is through the life experiences of others. We need not, and cannot, have every experience ourselves. We learn by what happens to us, of course, but we also learn by the reports of what happens to others—reports of success and reports of failure, of joys and sorrows, of lessons learned. Spiritual wills can help us find a path through the wilderness of our individual lives.

Spiritual wills can also mitigate the losses inflicted by time. There are people from the past whose lives could benefit ours. Who does not wish they knew more about some past family member? We long not just for biographical facts but also for a glimpse of their values and vision. That suffragette great-great-aunt, that circuit preacher great-grandfather. We would not only enjoy knowing what they thought, but we would also be better for knowing it. Similarly, who might benefit from our spiritual will in the future? Perhaps some great-grandchild we will never meet but who will be blessed by our spiritual legacy—maybe in the form of a spiritual will.

The following example, from Julie Anderson Friesen, a woman in her forties, is addressed to college-age students whom she does not know. I had asked her to speak to a class I was teaching about a legacy question that is good for anyone to answer: what is a good life? She was not able to come to the class, but sent the following letter:

> Dear Dan,
>
> Sorry I won't be there tomorrow. I was already starting to love your students in a sort of abstract way, and have been thinking about them all month—and also praying for them. I remember what they are going through: the insecurity, the impending drift that happens after college, the doubts and the uncertainties about jobs and relationships, the grieving that goes on when you leave a community—let alone the cocoon of friendship and accountability and terra firma at a place like Bethel. Yet, they've

also nearly had enough—their wings are itching. They want to claim their place in the world—but where is it?

So, please tell your class that the shape of a good life in the next five years may likely include suffering, and disappointment, and that horrible feeling that other friends' lives seem to be taking shape while theirs feels like a flat tire. Others have been there before them—and eventually the teeter will totter the other direction and things will start to take shape, though it may be in fits and starts. (In the mean time, I would encourage them not to use relationships with the opposite sex as a crutch. It wastes time and energy and produces regret.)

I also know that right now they are spending lots of time trying to divine God's will in their lives and are likely second-guessing everything from where to live, to who to marry, to how in the world their major is going to provide them a job in this economy—and maybe even dreading the very real possibility that they will need to move home. They imagine everyone else having it more figured out than they do, but the ones who do seem to have it figured out are usually standing behind a very thin façade. They are going about their day texting and checking Facebook and talking, but I know that at the back of their minds they are fretting and wondering and not really very peaceful. I ache for them.

So, I'd like to offer them the single most freeing truth that I learned while at Bethel, and it came from Chet Wood, my theology professor. My literature classes were critical for me in more ways than I can describe, but this one class, A Theology of Mission, gave me the key to peace and serenity during a time of great insecurity in college, and relieved the burden, as I've said, of second guessing God's will.

In studying a theology of mission from Old Testament through New, we were taught very clearly that God operated on a system of obedience and blessing. If I had to sum up my beliefs on the shape of a good life, it would indeed describe at least a God-fearing life as a shape with lots of open possibilities on the inside and a perimeter around it. Free will, within boundaries. Or maybe more like a river with all kinds of opportunities for delight, pain, suffering, abundance, adventure, and joy, but with banks. Disobedience runs you over the banks of the river and takes you out of the stream. You will wonder where the blessing is and life will be very, very dry. I know because I've been there—and the way back is always, always, always obedience.

But back to Chet Wood. He explored in meticulous detail the lives and stories of Abraham, Moses, Paul, and many others about the Biblical mandate for obedience and the promise of blessing. I realized for the first time that I could let my shoulders drop down from around my ears and that all the paths ahead of me held the promise for blessing! I could choose any one of them, as long as I pursued obedience—and God would bless that path. It was so freeing!

There wasn't one person I was supposed to marry, one mystery career that I had to figure out like a game of Clue, one city I was destined to live in, one job I was supposed to take. The pressure was off! God was abundant and I saw all opportunities as a buffet of God's blessings. When I chose one, and when I sought Him, when I stayed in dialogue with Him, when I faced choices and stayed obedient, then God could really make some use of me and I would feel joy and purpose. Ahh, the peace! Shantih, shantih! Not Shazam, not Shamwow—but real Shalom!

So, I encourage these God-seeking hungry minds who were smart enough to sign up for a class with you and to be reflective enough to think about living a good life to celebrate the talents and frailties that God has bestowed uniquely upon them—the desires and dreams their Creator placed in their heart, their idiosyncratic passions and the interests that specifically engage them and make them feel enthused (in the truest sense of the word—en Theos)—and just follow their noses.

Over the years I've been an on-air radio announcer, an ad agency copywriter, a creative director, a television show host, a business owner, a college instructor, and even a part-owner of a baseball team. When I left college I didn't envision any of that. I didn't even know I wanted to do any of that. My parents didn't think I could do any of that. Some of it I don't want to do any more! And I think there's a lot ahead of me I haven't even imagined yet.

But though I've struggled to be obedient, God has always kept his promise. I've been blessed with more than I will ever deserve, and I'm not talking about money, but about a richly interesting life (at least to me—though I do live in South Dakota, so how hard can it be?). I've had unexpectedly serendipitous moments (like dinners out with Bill Murray) and creative work to do that doesn't compromise my integrity, a multitude of opportunities to serve a needy and broken world in Jesus's name, and a whole host of family and friends who are willing to let me share this grand adventure (with all of its beauty and terror) and who, miraculously, usually love me back.

If I were there to offer a benediction I would have led us all in the beautiful hymn, sung in a very Irish manner, which is my own personal fight song in life: Be Thou My Vision. The lyrics say it all.

Love,

Your favorite and most brilliant student ever, Julie A.

This is a spiritual will, again in letter form, that is intended as a blessing for people the writer does not know. But in another sense, she does know them, because she has been in their shoes. And so she writes with compassion as well as wisdom about the questions they face in life, hoping to be of help.

Rachael Freed distinguishes between "instructions" and "blessings" in giving others advice about how to live. There is certainly teaching going on in spiritual wills, but they work best when the teaching feels more like a blessing, as here, than like operating instructions.

Historically, spiritual legacies have more often been in letter form than any other. Some even refer to this form as "legacy letters." Because letters are usually directed to an individual, and are naturally intimate, the letter may be the easiest form to use in trying to pass legacy wisdom on to another.

The Time to Create a Spiritual Will

When is the time to create a spiritual will? The answer is easy—now. And it has a follow-up—again later. You should write a spiritual will as soon as you think you have learned anything about life, and as soon as you can imagine someone who might profit from hearing what you've learned. Since everyone has learned something, and since you, at the very least, can benefit yourself from putting it down in writing, then clearly now is the time to create one.

None of the expected excuses hold water:

"I'm too young."

You are not too young to have core values, to have had life experiences, to have some tentative thoughts about what is important. Nor are you too young to have people in your life who would love to know what makes you tick, what you are thinking, how you see the world. You are also, unfortunately, not too young to die in the next twenty-four hours. So put something of yourself in writing, a legacy for now and for the future.

"I'm too old."

Too old to be a blessing to someone you love? Too old to think about the significance of your long life? The older you are the more you have to write about. Your problem is having too much to say, not too little. Besides, being old can only be followed by two possibilities: getting older still or dying. Both of these can preclude the kind of lucidity necessary to write what is on one's heart, as a nineteenth-century writer of a spiritual will understood: "Who knows whether I shall be clear-minded when my time comes and responsible for my actions. I have decided, therefore, to plan my journey now."

"I'm too tired."

Thinking requires very few calories. If you have enough energy to watch television, you have enough energy to create a spiritual will.

"I'm too busy."

Here is a three-word response to this universal three-word alibi for evading important callings: wood, hay, stubble. That's the biblical assessment of a great many of the things that make up our busyness. One of the spiritual wills that follows was written in ten minutes. Think of what you could accomplish in a couple of hours. A spiritual will is the perfect spiritual legacy format for people who think they are too busy.

"I don't have anything to say."

You have lots to say; you may simply not yet know how to say it. That's the job of this book. Keep reading.

"My life is not important."

Congratulations. You have just insulted God and everyone who has ever needed you (make a list of the latter). That's accomplishing a lot with just a few words. It is, as we have seen, the fundamental conviction of all spiritual legacy work that every single life is valuable and revelatory. It is arrogant, ironically, for you to think you are the exception.

So much for the excuses—what are some of the occasions for writing a spiritual will? The responsibility in the last third of life to pass on wisdom is, of course, one such occasion. Social psychologists speak of "generativity"—the felt need to contribute something to the well-being of the larger community, especially for the benefit of the next generation. Most of us struggle for decades in the pursuit of *success*, and then our focus shifts to seeking *significance*. There is no better way to be significant than to leave a legacy of insight and blessing.

But the last third of life is only one ripe time for doing legacy work. As Baines points out, spiritual wills are appropriate for any time of transition: marriage, the birth of a child or grandchild, changing careers, entering middle age, accomplishing something, retiring. They are also fitting in times of pain: divorce, loss of a loved one, when facing a health or other crisis, loss of a job. Anything that reminds you of core truths about what is important in life is a prompt for doing spiritual legacy work, including a spiritual will.

And this is not something that you do just once. When you have written something, take it out periodically—perhaps at the next transition or celebration or crisis—and see if you have any arguments with your previous self. What would you like to add? What are you inclined to change? What do you believe more strongly than ever? Revise an existing spiritual will, or better, leave it as a record of a particular time and now write another one. No one will be shocked if life causes you to change your mind here and there.

How to Create a Spiritual Will: Guided Reflection

The first step to creating a spiritual will is guided reflection—with a pen or keyboard at hand. You can't pass something on to another in a spiritual will until you know what it is yourself (and the action of creating it often helps you *discover* and *clarify* for yourself what you know and believe).

Here are some exercises to provide that guidance.

EXERCISE ONE

A. Make a list of three (or more) single-word values or virtues that are important to you. (Consult, if you wish, the "Values, Virtues, and Valuables" list in the appendix.) These do not have to be your three highest, just three you might want to include in a spiritual will. A sense of humor, for instance, might be important to you, even if it isn't your highest value.

Example: *perseverance, curiosity, compassion*

B. Choose one of the three and define it in your own words. Don't try to sound like a dictionary. Define it in the way that makes it meaningful to you, and in the way you speak.

Example: *Compassion, for me, means feeling someone else's pain enough to want to do something about it.*

C. Then write a brief, informal discussion of it. Expand on your definition and discuss why it is an important value to you.

Example: *Compassion is more than just feeling sorry for somebody. It's a feeling sorry that motivates me to do something, even if it is only to be with a person while he or she is suffering. I think modern life tends to kill compassion. We are encouraged to look out for number one. We tend to see other people's problems as a drain on our time and energy. We watch stories of crime victims on television for entertainment. Urban life encourages us to look the other way. I want to be a person who says, "If that were happening to me, I'd want some help." I want to be that help. I also want to be someone who will accept help when I need it.*

D. Story it. Look for a story from your own life that embodies something of what you want to convey about that value or virtue. What life experience first made you aware of it or taught you something about it? When have you succeeded, or failed, in modeling it yourself?

Example: *As a teacher, I know I have both succeeded and failed in showing compassion in my professional life. I once heard back from a woman who had been my advisee a number of years earlier. She reminded me of when, as a freshman, she came into my office at my request to discuss a failing grade she was receiving in another teacher's class. She was devastated by her failure, was sure her college career was over, and expected me to tell her how unfit she was as a student and human being. Instead, I had told her that she was not the first person to receive an F, that it was not the end of the world, that it said something about her performance in this one class at this particular time, but it didn't define her as a person, and that it could be overcome. At the time, I thought it just a typical conversation about a typical problem with a typical student. She let me know years later that the exchange was a turning point in her life.*

On the other hand, I also once ran into a student twenty-five years later who said, "You disrespected my story in your class," and it was clear that the wound was still fresh. Two stories—both about compassion, both worth telling.

E. Now, armed with all this raw material, write something about the value or virtue that could be included in your spiritual will.

This first exercise starts with one of the particular pieces that might go into a spiritual will. You can also start with big questions—very big questions—such as the following:

EXERCISE TWO

A. Answer one or more of the following (consult the "Spiritual Legacy Questions" in the appendix for more):

1. What did you once believe was important that you no longer believe to be so important? What caused you to change your mind?

2. What did you once not think important that you now consider more so? What from your life caused the change?

3. On September 11, 2001, many people made last calls from doomed airplanes and burning offices to those they loved. If you had to make that call, what would you want to say, and to whom?

4. Envision a great-grandchild that you will never meet who needs to know something about you. What do you want them to know about you? About life?

5. How do you see God differently now than you once did? Why?

B. Use parts of your answers in creating your spiritual will.

Another way to generate material is to focus on important characters in your own life.

EXERCISE THREE

A. Take the values list you created in exercise 1, part A. Expand the list to include more values and virtues that are particularly important to you. (Again, consult the "Values, Virtues, and Valuables" in the appendix if you wish.)

B. Create a list of important people from your past and present, emphasizing those who have influenced you in a positive way. The list will include many you know personally, but can also include people long dead whom you never met, even some you have only known through books.

C. Compare the two lists you have just created. What person on your list embodies a value or virtue in the other list? Who has taught you something important? Who has modeled some value (or failed to do so in an instructive way)? For example, if moral courage is a high value for you, whom do you know who has shown it?

D. Construct part of a spiritual will by writing about the intersection of your two lists.

Yet another way of generating material for a spiritual will is to reflect on its recipient. You aren't required to know whom a spiritual will is for—it can be "To whomever this may concern"—but if you do know, thinking about that person or persons can help you know what you want to say. You may say things to one person that you would not say to another.

EXERCISE FOUR

A. Make a list of those you would particularly like to benefit from your spiritual will. It can be someone you know well, someone you would like to know better, or even someone who is not yet born and whom you may never meet.

B. Beside each name, write thoughts about that person's life—their present life or perhaps their future. Where are they in life—developmentally, psychologically, physically, intellectually, spiritually? What do you value about them? Why do you like them? What about them makes you smile? What do you think they need? What would help them live more fully? What would make them happier?

C. Create a blessing for them. It might be in the form of a prayer for them (see Num. 6:23–26) or simply words that wish them well. Make it specific to them.

D. Write a series of "May you . . ." or "I hope for you . . ." sentences, completing each in a way that addresses a different part of their lives (from career and finances to family and faith). Be creative. Humorous blessings and hopes are also good.

E. Use this material in creating your spiritual will.

As we have seen, a good strategy for generating material for a spiritual will is using sentence-completion and cataloging exercises. A beginning phrase, such as "I am thankful for . . ." or "I love . . ." or "I believe . . ." (the credo approach), can be completed in an infinite number of ways, all revealing something about the one who completes it.

A catalog is a list of items that share something in common. Walt Whitman used cataloging in his poetry to celebrate and embrace the teeming life of New York. You can use it to explore the richness of your own life.

EXERCISE FIVE

A. Create a list of sentence openings that call for completion. In addition to the three openings above, here are some others, each of which can be used to create a separate catalog or list (you can also come up with some of your own):

—"I hope people say (will say) that I . . ."
—"My mission/calling/joy is to . . ."
—"I want my life to show . . ."
—"Fun/Beauty/Courage/etc. is . . ."
—"My life will be a success if . . ."
—"I hope for you . . ."
—"I am indebted to (name) for teaching me that . . ."
—"I will always try to . . ."
—"If I had it to do over again, I would . . ."
—"What I value most is . . ."

B. Choose one and complete the sentence in as many different ways as occur to you. Use the same opening words throughout the list.

C. Choose some of those completed sentences and write more about them, perhaps linking them to individuals and stories.

D. Use this material in your spiritual will.

In many of the above exercises it can help to think in various categories: relationships, career/professional life, family life/marriage/ parenting, spiritual life, hobbies or passions.

The Structure of a Spiritual Will

Once you have got a start on what you might want to say, you need to think about how to say it. The good news is that it doesn't matter. There is no single structure for a spiritual will. It does not need to be eloquent or crafted or stylistically impressive.

And you do not have to know *everything* you want to say before you start. Beginning to write is something like trying to start a fire. At first it is a lot of fussing and no heat. But once you coax a spark or two into flame, you have the beginning of a fire that can burn down Rome. If you know even one thing you want to say, the process of saying it will reveal to you another. The person who claims he or she doesn't know what to say will become the person who has to be told to stop for the sake of the forests.

The spiritual will can take many forms. Here are three possibilities.

The Legacy Letter

As we have seen, the letter is the most natural form of legacy for many writers—and has been for centuries. The personal letter is intimate, flexible, and familiar. Anyone can begin a legacy letter as follows:

> Dear Rebecca,
> I would like to share some things that mean a lot to me and that I hope will be helpful to you.

Letters can be of any length, though if they get too long they start feeling like essays. They can also be written in a series and then collected together. You can write different letters on different topics. You can also write different legacy letters to different people, having some common material, but tailoring the rest to the specific recipient.

Some people write annual letters that serve a legacy purpose. A letter each Christmas or New Year to a growing child, for instance, can give an overview of his or her life that past year, offering reflections on it and on the year to come, and passing on insights and blessings as seem fitting. A collection of such letters would be a powerful record of a childhood, with the potential to shape life as an adult.

The Essay

The personal essay can be as intimate and flexible as the letter and is even better suited to prolonged reflection. An essay displays a mind ruminating on a topic—any topic. In an essay you can range far and wide, bringing in material from others, transitioning from one subject to another, exploring equally what you think and how you feel.

An essay might be a good choice if you do not have anyone in particular in mind for your spiritual will. You are making a statement about life as you see it—your life and life in general—and the essay is a natural form for such statements.

The essay lends itself to storytelling as well as to reflection. You can easily tell stories from your own life and then reflect on them, probing them for what they have to teach. If stories begin to predominate, however, then you are moving toward a "story legacy" (see following chapters) more than a spiritual will. Ultimately, of course, it doesn't matter what you call it; what matters is what you learn about your own life and who you bless.

The List

Perhaps the simplest form of all for a spiritual will is the list. Think Ten Commandments. A list can be a numbered series of assertions or principles or commands or value statements or questions or anything else that lends itself to the goal of passing on wisdom and blessings. (For instance, your own version of the Ten Commandments.)

One traditional form of this is the credo—a word meaning "I believe." What do you believe—about anything? Start a list of "I believes," as in exercise 5. Range through different areas of human experience: relationships, business, faith, attitudes in life, politics, the arts, and the like. If you keep strictly to the list form, you won't have much room for storytelling or lengthy reflection. But you can cover a lot of ground in a short space.

Lists can seem impersonal if unadorned, but there is nothing to prevent you from including a warm opening and closing, personal comments within the list, and references to the recipient's life. You can have a single list or break it into subcategories.

The following is an example of a spiritual will that combines two approaches, offering a list within a letter. Should the writer wish, he could easily expand this into an essay form as well, giving more of his thoughts on each imperative. This was written as a response to question 3 in exercise 2 above, concerning what the writer would want to say to a loved one if he had only minutes to live. It was written by a middle-aged man, William Weld-Wallis, to his wife.

> To Tess:
> Tell the kids to love peace and reconciliation, and to work toward it. I learned that from Martin Luther King.
>
> Tell them to choose the way of Jesus because it offers the best way to live, not because it offers the easiest way to eternal life. I learned that from William Stringfellow.
>
> Tell them to find Christ in all things. I learned that from St. Ignatius.
>
> Tell them to find meaning in the Eucharist. I learned that from the Plymouth Brethren, the Episcopalians, and, finally, from Bishop Oscar Romero.
>
> Tell them to embrace our culture, loving what is creative and life giving, but naming what is seductive, diseased, and immoral. I learned that from Fr. John Staudenmaier, SJ, and from contemporary prophets and artists (even some here at Trinity Church!).
>
> Tell them that fidelity, in love and in faith, is honorable, and that it is possible even in a culture that teaches that nothing can be permanent. I learned that from Fr. John Kavanaugh, SJ.
>
> Tell them that God has a preferential option for the poor. I learned that from our brothers and sisters in Latin America.
>
> Tell them to learn, to expand their experiences and their minds. I learned that first from my parents, and then from the many educators, professors, pastors, and friends who have pushed and challenged me.
>
> Tell them that I love them.
>
> Tell them that I love you.
> > Bill

Please note some things about this spiritual will:

1. It is short, created in ten minutes, plus a few minutes of revision later.
2. It is simple—a series of straightforward, unelaborated imperative and declarative sentences, all starting with the same phrase. No

high language or attempt to sound profound, though the letter is profound.

3. It is specific. Not vague generalities, but a handful of related core values and practices. It ties each abstract value or virtue to a specific person.

4. It is tied to the writer's life and to people in his life, including people he never met.

5. It doesn't try to say everything, focusing instead on a central theme of his life and convictions. There's plenty more he can say, perhaps in a separate piece of legacy work, but this feels complete in itself and can stand alone.

6. It is not all that much about him as an individual. It tells us indirectly who he is by telling us what he values, but it is not self-absorbed or self-probing.

7. It is not sentimental, but it is filled with love.

8. It is full of wisdom—a lifetime of it in just a few words.

9. It would be a great thing to receive from someone who cared about you.

10. It has value even for someone who will never know the writer.

Further Guidelines

Don't put a lot of pressure on yourself to create the definitive statement about the meaning of life. You are simply passing on a few thoughts in a few words (not condensing the Bible).

Feel free to be lighthearted and playful. Tell jokes if you wish.

Add objects if it seems fitting: photographs, music, memorabilia, original art or reproductions.

If you don't feel you have any answers, create a list of great questions.

Feel free in a later spiritual will to contradict what you said in an earlier one.

Use the words of others: favorite poems or quotations, song lyrics, lines from movies, Bible verses—especially if you can connect them to your own experience.

Feel free to ask and give forgiveness.

Do not use it as a place to get even, preach sermons, shake your finger, scold, or speak badly of someone else.

Keep it fairly short. A few things said well are more powerful (and likely to be read) than a rambling dissertation.

Pay attention to tone. Think tone of voice. Avoid sounding harsh or schoolmarmish or pontifical or lecturing. Try for a tone that is inviting, engaging, openhanded, and affirming. Let grace, not law, be the dominant voice.

Remember Solzhenitsyn's warning that a last word of parting may be how you are imprinted on the minds of those who love you and wish you well. Make that word (even if it isn't a last one) an encouraging word.

Avoid clichés, platitudes, and slogans.

Speak from your own life. Give examples from it.

Write more than one spiritual will—write at various stages in life, on various topics and occasions, and to various people.

Write for your own benefit—to clarify your life—as well as for others.

Last Words

I will end with one last example of a spiritual will. This is written by a woman, Betty Eleanor Lowther, who had recently been diagnosed with Alzheimer's. She asked that it be read to the family in her last hours. It addresses the past, present, and future and is written for her children and grandchildren. It speaks for itself.

> To My Beloved Children,
>
> My deepest and greatest love will always be surrounding each of you, whether we are together or separated for a time. You know and I know that God does have a purpose for each of our lives. I am finding out that His Purpose and our purpose may not be the same.
>
> I have been brought face to face with my own mortality. There is no cure for Alzheimer's except death. It is a turning point for each of us in a sense. I have made it a point to be as realistic about facing my death as possible. Because of my faith in God, I will not fear death. On the contrary, I will welcome it

because at that point I will be reunited with my Beloved—your Beloved father. And with other family members of mine who have proceeded me. I am looking forward to our Reunion in Heaven—God's Kingdom.

My heart will ache for you, our children and grandchildren, because it will be more difficult for you as your second parent goes home to God. The pain will pass as you concentrate on the good memories. When this hard part comes, try to rejoice with Dad and me that we are reunited. And always remember it is our prayer that each of you will choose to accept our Lord, Jesus Christ as your Personal Savior, so that as your turn comes you may have the privilege of being reunited with us, in God's Kingdom forever and ever, never again to be parted.

As my last breath comes, remember that between that split second and the next Dad and I are reunited—never again to part. Always concentrate on the good memories we have shared through the years. Nothing, not even death, can take those from you. Earth is a proving ground, I do believe, that prepares us for Heaven. Always remember you will still have the full measure and depth of our love, even though we are temporarily separated. We have shared a powerful Christian Heritage all these years, and I do believe that the best is yet to be when we are all reunited in God's Kingdom.

Most importantly, remember your heritage. We have all been truly blessed to be a family unit and we will continue to be that unit in Heaven—that Home above where there will be no sorrow, no pain, no heartache, just Love, Love, Love, as God intended it to be.

I can honestly say I'm anxious to be reunited with your Dad, my parents, brothers, grandparents, great grandparents—all who have preceded me. I can assure you, the Heavenly Hosts that are waiting are the greatest I know. I like to think about how happy your Dad must have been when he was reunited with his parents, especially his mother, because he was only thirteen when she went to her Eternal Home.

I ask that you will continue to make the best of the future by making time to be together as family, by building new memories to cherish as you rejoice that Dad and I are reunited. We

will surround you with our prayers for your blessings forever.
Our deepest prayers will always be with you wherever you are.

Remember me with joy and laughter and with the memories
of the happy times we shared as a family and with friends.

With all my love always and forever.

Mom

Writing a spiritual will requires nothing more than the willingness
to do so. There are very few things you can do in life that have a greater
return for the amount of effort required. What are you waiting for?

3

Story Legacies

A lifestory is a gift one generation bestows upon another, a legacy
people have been giving from the beginning of time.

Denis Ledoux

You *are* your stories. Our identity is formed largely by the stories we
tell ourselves, in conjunction with those told to us by others. It is good
to state your values and insights for those you care about in a spiritual
will, as we explored in the previous chapter. It is even better to tell the
stories out of which those values and that wisdom arose. Stories give
flesh and blood, emotions, and all the colorful bits and pieces of real
life to the abstractions and distillations that we call values and virtues.
Abstractions engage our minds. Stories engage everything about us—
mind, emotions, spirit, imagination, body, and more. Therefore nothing
in life has more power to shape us than stories.

We leave a littered trail of things behind us as we meander through
life—degrees, titles, jobs, houses, possessions, even spouses and friends.
All of these are part of my life, but none of them is *me*—a uniquely

51

created being, one never created before and never to be created again. Is there any part of my life that can endure, that can be preserved, for my own sense of significance and for the benefit of others? The closest thing we have to a more permanent existence is our stories. Our stories capture more of who we are and what our life has been than anything else in the human experience.

Stories are, among other things, organisms for storing and preserving a life. But they do not do so in a static, mothballed way. Stories do not preserve our lives in the same way that mummification preserves a body or quite in the way that a battery preserves a charge. Rather, stories preserve a life in the way a plant preserves the sun. They absorb and embody the energy and dynamism of a life as a tree ties up the energy of the sun in its limbs, ready to be released again should someone strike a match.

Why Stories?

We explored in chapter 1 why stories are so well suited to convey the intricacies of human experience. They entangle the details of events, characters, decisions, quandaries, judgments, and outcomes that make our life experience. By giving it the shape of a plot—a beginning, middle, and end—they make it both memorable and accessible. We have a natural ability to interpret data that comes to us in story form. Present a life to us as a story and we have a much better chance of making sense of it.

Essentially, stories are the only form of human expression that begins to match the complexity and diversity of experience itself. And they are the key to understanding and finding meaning in that experience. We know who we are in large part by understanding the stories that make up our lives. This is true for making sense of our own stories, but it is also true for benefiting from someone else's. This is one of the great blessings of the story enterprise. We can take pleasure in and wisdom away from the stories of others. Hence the power of story legacies.

Stories are fundamental to human well-being. We literally can't be human without them, because stories are what tell us what it means to be human in the first place. A helpful story is a gift that blesses both the teller and the receiver, and the best thanks for such a gift is to tell a story in return. Or to pass the story on.

The Five Convictions of Story Legacies

There are many convictions, stated and unstated, that underlie the exhortation to share your legacy in the form of stories. Here are five of them:

EVERYONE HAS A STORY WORTH TELLING.

There are no exceptions to this. To think otherwise is an insult to God and to those who have shared your life. The notion that "my life is not important" or "I don't have any stories worth sharing" is either false modesty or obtuseness. Your stories are not important because you are important (though you are); your stories are important because they have the potential to help someone else.

EVERYONE HAS THE RIGHT TO TELL IT.

The mid-twentieth-century Italian novelist Ignazio Silone said everyone has the right to tell their own story in their own ways. It is, I would add, a right we grant even to the most heinous criminals—the right to tell in court their side of the story however they choose. Not to allow people a voice, an opportunity to express their own experience and how they feel about it, is a form of oppression that we have seen many times in history. This is one right that we have an *obligation* to exercise.

EVERYONE HAS THE RESPONSIBILITY TO PASS ON WISDOM.

This is the core conviction of this book. You do not have the right to keep what you have learned to yourself. Others shared their wisdom with you, at every stage of your life, and it's your responsibility, not just your right, to do the same.

Even when you are young, you are responsible to share what you know with those who need to know it—and you will never fully know who needs it or when (perhaps a friend now, perhaps someone in the next generation). Even if you have not come to many conclusions about what your life experiences mean, you can share the experiences and reflect on them with what insight you have now. And the act of telling and reflecting will itself generate insight and help clarify your life for you.

And as you age, passing on wisdom is increasingly the primary responsibility of your life. You spend decades accumulating insights, often painfully won, and you should spend decades sharing them with those who need them. Sociologists point out that passing on wisdom is the main task of the last third of one's life, part of the shift, as we saw in the last chapter, from a focus on *success* to a focus on *significance*. But it can and should be done at any age. Have you learned something—even tentatively? Pass it on.

This doesn't require you to understand everything, not even within your own life. Some legacy work is simply preserving the experience, leaving until later (and maybe for others) to assess more fully what the experience signifies. Your job is not to be all knowing (that job is taken); it is to preserve and reflect and share.

Stories are the single best way to do so.

I have already tried to make the case for this in the opening chapter. Stories, both those preserved in memory and those freshly created, are the natural carriers of human experience and human values. They engage every part of us—mind, spirit, emotions, body. Tell me what to believe and I may or may not agree. Tell me a story and I will absorb and live with it.

My hope is that the particular stories you discover in this book will ease any doubts you have about using stories to pass on wisdom. If you have found a better way, then use it, but for the same goals.

Everyone has the ability to tell their own stories.

Even those who agree with the first four assertions often resist this last one, but it is absolutely true. "Telling stories is for writers and storytellers. For word people. That's not me." Of course it's you. You get up telling stories, eat meals telling stories, do your work telling stories, and go to bed telling stories. Telling stories is as natural as breathing, and if the story grows out of your own life, you can even tell it with flair.

People are naturally articulate about their own stories. They may have no words in other situations, but ask them to tell about something that has happened to them and the story tells itself, often in a powerful way.

I once was standing outside church when an acquaintance walked up to me and said, "I have a shot at a five-minute radio spot, and I want to tell a story, but I can't tell stories—can you help me?" I replied, "What's the story?" He spent the next five minutes telling me the story, with passion and panache. I said to him, "I think you can tell that story—you just did." He looked stunned. "I guess I did, didn't I?" He spun on his heels and walked away, and that was the last I heard of it.

He could tell his story because it was *his* story, and because he cared about it, and because he wanted it to do his listeners some good. That makes all of us as articulate as we need to be.

This is more true of oral storytelling than of written, for reasons we will explore. But the differences are largely mental and practical. Writing down the stories you already tell—and some that you haven't yet even told to yourself—requires only willingness and a few practical suggestions, which this book will provide.

Biblical Story Legacies

If there are biblical models for spiritual wills—Jacob in Genesis 49 and Jesus at the Last Supper—there are also biblical models for telling stories and leaving story legacies. The Bible is many things, among them a great storybook dedicated to the cause of remembering well in order to live well and be a blessing to coming generations. The master plot of the Bible is something like this: God made you, God loves you, and God calls you. And that message is worked out in the details of hundreds of Bible stories.

The Gospels are collections of the stories of the life of Jesus, given to us so that we may learn and believe. Within those stories, Jesus himself tells a series of parables, another kind of story designed specifically to pass on wisdom. The book of Acts is the story of the founding and spreading of the church. The epistles are something different, but they too are full of stories and constantly refer back to the essential gospel story. And the book of Revelation ties the stories of the past and present together with the stories of the future.

Or consider Moses. When he learned in the book of Deuteronomy that he would not be allowed to enter the promised land, what did he do? He assembled the nation of Israel and told them stories of their past together in order to prepare them for their future. He told them stories of failure and of success, of obedience and of disobedience, of times when they were close to God and of times when they wandered away.

Moses was not telling Israel these stories to entertain them, or to pass the time until he walked up the mountain to die. He told them these stories because they needed them. They needed to remember their stories in order to remember who they were and what they should do. Without their stories, they literally did not know themselves or how to live.

The Bible, like all sacred texts, understands that storytelling is the primary vehicle for preserving and passing on faith. It roots itself in history and in recounting the actions of God in time and space. Israel is called to faith not in an abstract concept called God but in the God who "rescued you out of Egypt," that is, in the God who acts—as recorded in stories. We are called to do the same—to tell the stories of, among many things, God acting in our lives.

Stories, however, are never more than one generation from extinction. If they are not repeated, they die. And they cannot be repeated until they are formed in the first place. This is why the Bible is filled with so many admonitions to tell the stories, especially to the children. In the third and fourth chapters of the book of Joshua, the people of Israel have a new storyteller and interpreter of the story. Joshua has replaced Moses, whose story has ended on the mountaintop.

Moses has died, and it is Joshua's job to get many thousands of people across the Jordan River. The river, however, is at flood stage, much too wide and swift for a crossing. But God tells Joshua he is going to put on a show, so that people will have as much confidence in their new leader Joshua as they had in Moses. God tells Joshua to have the priests carrying the ark of the covenant to step into the river. When they do, the river "heaps" up (so the Hebrew tells us) and the priests walk into the now-dry riverbed and stand in the middle until all the people have passed over to the other side.

God then tells Joshua to have a representative from each of the twelve tribes go to the place where the priests are standing with the ark and for each of them to take a stone from the middle of the river and carry it to the other side. Those stones are piled into a monument "to serve as a sign among you. In the future, when your children ask you, 'What do these stones mean?' tell them that the flow of the Jordan was cut off before the ark of the covenant of the LORD. When it crossed the Jordan, the waters of the Jordan were cut off. These stones are to be a memorial to the people of Israel forever" (Josh. 4:6–7 NIV).

This is a passage about the importance of legacy and of story.

The nation of Israel had a problem with memory lapses. The prophets (who were essentially storytellers) were always telling them to remember the stories of the past because they were the key to the present and future. When the people remembered who they were, where they had come from, and who their God was, they prospered. When they quit telling the stories, they no longer knew who they were and they invited disaster.

This is why Joshua ordered each of the tribes of Israel to contribute a rock to commemorate God's provision for them in leading them across the River Jordan into the promised land. The rock monument in their midst will act as a story prompt. It will cause the children of the next generation, who didn't themselves witness the event, to ask why those rocks are there. The children's question will prompt the story—and a new generation will understand the power of God. The story is quite explicit about this: "He did this so that all the peoples of the earth might know that the hand of the LORD is powerful and so that you might always fear the LORD your God" (Josh. 4:24 NIV).

This story is a powerful and important reminder for the Israelites who experienced it and a legacy for those who followed, including us. It reminds the Israelites who they are and who their God is, and it passes on that wisdom to the next generation. This is what a spiritual legacy does. It grows out of actual experience in a person's or community's life, it contains some important truth about living, and it conveys that truth to someone who needs it.

The Bible is especially concerned that the children and the next generation are steeped in the stories and the wisdom they convey. In one passage among many, the psalmist tells the story of his suffering and of God's compassionate response and then commands that this story and this truth be passed on (Ps. 102:18, my translation):

> Let this be recorded for a future generation,
> that a people yet to be born may praise the LORD.

Who is this "future generation" for which the story has been preserved? It's you and me.

How is it that we have the opportunity to know the God who created us? Because someone told the story. And someone else wrote down the story. And others chose to repeat the story. And many were willing to die for the story. And so generation after generation, the story of God's love for his creation has been told—and we are the beneficiaries.

Which raises the question, are we going to be the generation that stops passing on the story?

And what is true in the story of God's compassion for the psalmist is also true in the story of God's compassion for you. You have stories that need telling, and there are people who need to hear them.

You and I can say with the psalmist:

> O God, You have taught me since I was young,
> and I still declare Your wondrous deeds.
> Even when I am old and gray,
> do not abandon me, my God,
> until I declare your power to the next generation,
> your mighty acts to all who are to come. (Ps. 71:17–18,
> my translation)

Notice that every age group is mentioned here. The speaker acknowledges God's teaching in youth, seems to be speaking now in middle age, and asks for strength to continue telling the stories in the future even when old and gray. No matter where you are in life, you have stories to tell that someone else needs to hear.

Moses, David, the prophets, Matthew, Mark, Luke, John, Peter, Paul—all storytellers. And Jesus more than any of them, because he lives and tells the story that makes sense of all stories. We must pass on their stories, but we must also tell how their stories have shaped our own. This is our responsibility and joy. (And if your stories of faith involve doubt and struggle and failure, tell them honestly, for the Bible is full of those stories as well, and they too have their wisdom.)

Stories with Reflection and Without

One should not talk about story without telling stories. These stories serve not as formulas for how to write or what to write about, but simply as examples of ordinary people telling their stories in ways that clearly have something to offer the rest of us.

The following story shows how straightforward and spare an effective story can be.

It was written by a retired printer and inventor, Harold Paulsen, about his memories of growing up very poor in the 1920s and 30s in northern Minnesota. He tells us what happened but feels no need to tell us what he thought about it—then or now. He calls it, "The Indian that Couldn't Talk."

> The spring season had been very dry. The farmer's crops that had been planted didn't seem to germinate or sprout except in the low lands where there was surface moisture. It also was the year of the grasshoppers. There were so many that you couldn't see the ground in many places on the edge of the grain and cornfields. We spread poisoned bran to kill them. Many trees were completely stripped of their leaves and small twigs.
>
> We dreaded the hot summer heat and winds that would follow, because the weatherman had forecast this to be the year of the drought, grasshoppers, and 105-degree days. I remember a caravan of Indians traveling from White Earth to the Osage reservation. A young Indian woman dropped back into the swamp on the Andersen farm to have her baby. Soon after the birth, she and an older lady who may have been her mother

picked up the child and moved on to catch up with the tribe. We all marveled at the strength of these people.

The winter months were very hard because of the snow and the extreme cold. I remember our neighbor losing one of his beef cattle. The vet didn't know what it had died from, but he left instructions for the farmers to haul it off into the field, away from the rest of his livestock, to be buried in the spring. It was done just in case of a contagious disease.

The Indians that winter were having a hard time spearing fish for food in their teepee fish houses. They spotted the dead cow. The feet and head were sticking up through the snow. They asked the farmer if they could have it for food, so he gave it to them. We didn't hear of anyone getting sick from eating the meat. Maybe the frost killed the germs.

One night in February (I remember because we had celebrated my birthday with Pete and Aunt Leland the week before), Dad went to Blooming Prairie because his Mother, our Grandma Paulson, had passed away. It was about one in the morning and very cold. We had done the usual work of heating rocks and flat stones. We wrapped them in newspaper to keep them from burning our legs. This was the only way to keep our bed warm.

Mother came upstairs and scared us half-to-death by waking us up and telling us there was a man walking back and forth on the porch. And sure enough, when we got down there, we could see a figure in the door. As he took each step, you could hear the cold snow make a crunching noise. We crept very slowly to the window, keeping very low as we peered over the window ledge to see, of all things, a big Indian.

Lloyd immediately went for the sawed-off shotgun. This was the old shotgun that Peter Leland loaned us for crow hunting. He had previously stuck the barrel into the ground while crossing a fence and accidentally plugged the barrel. So when he aimed to shoot at a crow, the gun exploded, blowing six inches of the barrel off and knocking Peter to the ground. So he had given the gun to us.

The question now was what should we do? We knew that if he stayed out in the cold, he would freeze to death, so we decided to let him come in. Mother was very frightened, but we placed more wood on the fire in the kitchen stove so he could get warm. Lloyd was to sit back in the corner with that sawed-off shotgun to guard him. Up to this time, the Indian had not spoken one word.

We decided that Leonard and I would sleep on the floor in the living room next to the airtight heater, so that Mother would feel safe and get some rest. We had just begun to doze off when we heard a loud bang. Lloyd had fallen asleep and dropped the gun. It went off, missing his foot by an inch and blowing a hole in the kitchen floor. The echo sounded like a stick of dynamite exploding. We all jumped and ran for the kitchen. Mother was crying. She thought Lloyd had killed the Indian.

The Indian didn't move or say anything. Morning came and we fixed food for him—the usual oatmeal with some cattle farm bran, cow's milk and a piece of toast with goose grease and brown sugar. The Indian left as he came, without saying one word. That fall he returned with a bucket of wild raspberries at harvest time. He came back later with a bucket of wild rice, but still no words were spoken.

We figured he was so grateful that his life had been saved from the cold winter weather and also from the shotgun blast! Today as I write about this part of my life, I believe that the Lord's angels were looking after our family too, because that shotgun could have killed someone.

This is a good story. Like a lot of men his age, perhaps, the writer feels the story is enough; no need to chew on it beyond the observation that God spared them a tragedy. And he's right. The story itself reveals a great amount about how people survived, about relationships between the races, about human kindness mixed with wariness, about honor and reciprocity. It is informative, sad, humorous, and uplifting all at the same time. The writer does not have to point all this out; perhaps he does not see them all himself. Like all good writers, he is trusting the story.

A dusty piece of advice often given to writers of fiction says "show, don't tell." The idea is that revelations in stories come primarily through the actions of characters, not through pronouncements by the narrator. And it is generally good advice, though there are plenty of exceptions in good fiction.

It is not so with legacy work. The basic strategy of nonfiction prose, especially in life writing, is both to show *and* tell. Or, to put it another way, to *describe* and *reflect*. That is, one tells the story with the same tools of character and plot and scenes as used in fiction, but one is also allowed, often required, to reflect on the story.

Reflection takes many forms. Essentially it is any probing, chewing, analyzing, investigating, or pondering that the teller offers on the facts of the story. Sometimes it comes after the story; sometimes it is interwoven within the story; sometimes, as with the story of the Indian on the porch, it is largely absent.

As the teller of a story, you are free to reflect openly on it as much or as little as you like. Some stories are better left to stand on their own. But in legacy work your reflection may be as or more important than the story itself—in fact, your reflection *is part of* the story. The person to whom you are passing your stories wants to know what *you* think and feel about the story you are telling. Showing and telling go hand in hand.

Trust the story. Let it speak for itself. But also speak yourself *about* the story if you think it helpful. Often it will be.

If you find the idea of having to say something profound about one of your stories intimidating, don't worry about it. First, nobody is asking for profundity, just for your response to your own story. Second, reflection is optional.

In the story that follows, the facts of the story are given first, then the writer reflects eloquently on the significance of those facts. She is trying to make sense, for herself, of the story. She understands more of that significance now, as she tells the story, than she did at the time that the event took place. This is another reason to write down our stories—in the writing of them we may come to understand things that we had not fully understood when they happened.

This is a story by Amy Baker, a young woman in her mid-twenties, about something that will not let her go. She calls it, "Three Candles," and in the telling of this story, reflection on the central event is crucial.

Three candles . . . that's all she wanted. Just three candles.

I found myself speechless, as happens so often when I let being efficient and ordered and rule driven have priority over the needs of people. As I rushed toward her to stop her from painting too many candles, I wasn't thinking of her needs. I wasn't thinking about why she wanted so badly to paint those three little candles on the five-hundred-foot-long wall. I was only thinking about my needs. I was in charge of a giant community mural project in a South African township. I needed order, for everyone to follow the rules, to run a tight ship.

We agreed before starting: "Each person gets to paint only one candle in honor of someone they have lost to AIDS. If we just let anyone paint more than one candle, everyone will want to paint more than one candle . . . and we can't have that. We have to maintain some semblance of order here." Of course when we made "the rules," we hadn't considered that in Lower Crossroads one in three people is dying of AIDS. Most people who came to paint on the mural were going to know more than one person they would wish to honor on our wall.

My mission was clear—stop the young girl from painting more candles. She had already painted three before we had noticed. My motives were pure. There were only a few of us directing the work and so many people who wanted to paint. We needed to keep order. And order is a good thing . . . unless, that is, you forget people.

When I got to her, I nonchalantly sat next to her on the ground and said, "Hey, I see you're painting some beautiful candles. Who are they in honor of?" That sounds good, doesn't it? But truthfully, I wasn't interested in her answer. I was interested in stalling while I thought of a good way to tell her that her painting was done for the day.

She couldn't have been more than eighteen. She looked at me, held my gaze—unwavering, penetrating—then hesitated, as if trying to figure out if she could trust me with her answer.

When she spoke, she said simply, "This first one is for my husband, who died a year ago of AIDS. The second one is for my baby boy, who died eight months ago because of AIDS. The last one is for me . . . because I am dying, and it won't be long. I want my name on this wall. Thank you for letting me put my name on this wall."

I felt my heart drop to my ankles. My first thought was of my own failure. How terrible to let my need for control be more important than the people I was trying to reach out to. How even more terrible that this little one was faced with certain death at such a young age. How terrible her lost innocence, her pain. How terrible that some people never even get a fighting chance. Her unwavering gaze still haunts me.

She only wanted three candles. She only wanted her name on the wall. She only wanted to be remembered.

I still think about that girl. I wonder if she's alive and doing okay. I wonder how her spirit is and if anyone is taking care of her. I think about her candles. Don't they represent one of the most basic cries of our hearts? Isn't it something we all share? We all just want to be known by someone. We all just want to be remembered. We all want it to mean something that our feet have walked this soil, that we've laughed and cried here, that we've toiled and sweated here, that we've loved and been loved here. We want to know that we've made a difference for someone . . . anyone . . . here.

One of the things that breaks my heart in this world is knowing that some people have no one to help them feel their significance. They have no one to speak truth to them about their inherent value and worth in the arms of their creator. These people feel forgotten and invisible in the world. Imagine having no one to share your stories with, no one to fight for you, no one to speak your name into the air. All I know to do is to speak the names of these people, to tell their stories.

And the more I realize that I am, myself, quickly running out of minutes here, the more I understand this: we were made to be known and loved. We were made to have stories, real stories, full of both the joy and pain of living. We were made to share these stories with the world, and by doing so to change those around us.

I am not alone. We are all searching for significance in our own way. Whether it is the graffiti artists tagging train cars, my South African friend, the business man on Wall Street, the elementary school teacher, my grandpa or my niece, the screaming baby just delivered from the womb—we all want to know deep down that we matter to someone.

I will speak for myself. As I've faced death and my mortality, I've realized that I'm just like that South African girl. I want my name on a wall. I want to leave this life knowing that I wasn't a random blip on the radar screen, a cosmic accident. I want to know that my life means something to more than just me, that my fight to stay alive is worth it to someone else. And, after my life is done, at the end of the day, when it's time to say goodbye, I desperately want to know that people will still speak my name.

I am not naïve enough to think that we can go to these people and love the hurt off of them, or that we can fix all that is broken. But I do know this. We can write their names on a wall. We can speak their name and tell their stories, redeeming a small part of their painful lives and giving them dignity. We can tag this world with their beautiful spirits—one name at a time.

We can give them three candles—the three candles I want for myself.

It can be very helpful, in a spiritual will for instance, to tell someone that you believe compassion or dignity is important. But no abstract assertion is as powerful, memorable, and apt to change a life as a story that embodies the same message. This story of a woman dying of AIDS, told by a woman with serious threats to her own health, speaks to every part of us—our minds, our hearts, our emotions, our body, our imagination, our will, our spirit. The memory of this young African girl will not leave the writer alone, and the story will not leave us alone. It demands of us a response. It demands that we think and act differently. It is part of Amy's spiritual legacy, and now it is part of ours.

The teller of this story emphasizes the good we can do for others by speaking their names and telling their stories, and that is a central claim of this book. But it is clear that this story is also good for the teller. Within the African woman's story she finds her own. She finds that their stories are different versions of the same story, of a universal story, one in which we are all seeking significance for our lives.

This is how it is with spiritual legacy work. We do it for the benefit of others, but we cannot help but be blessed by it ourselves. John Donne wrote centuries ago that "no man is an island" and that the death of any one diminishes us all. We can also say, "No one lives their story alone." Our stories intermingle like currents in a stream. In telling my story, I am telling yours, or at least a story that can make yours better. And you can do the same for me.

It is worth noting that this story is written by a young woman. She has not lived long. She does not know, as none of us do, that she will live much longer. But she does know that significant things have already happened in her life and are happening every day. And so she puts them down in story form, a rock monument beside the Jordan, for the good of anyone who hears them.

Benefits of a Story Legacy

Preserving a Life

The most elemental benefit of telling a life story is the preservation of part of that life. Stories are life preservers, in many senses of the term. They save lives—literally and figuratively. A life is not an abstraction; it is a tangible organism existing in time and space. Because the body dies and decays and because time passes, any life is at risk of being lost—from time and space and memory. The single best protection against that oblivion is to tie up parts of that life in stories. Stories can endure long after bodies are gone. Telling a story saves a life. Why not yours?

The Power and Pleasure of Remembering

The past is where we live. In some senses, it is the only thing that exists—the future having not yet arrived and the present turning each instant into the past. The past is also the only unchanging thing in the universe. (Even God has new thoughts—they're called babies.) Our relation to it can change dramatically, but the past itself does not change. I admit this is only an approximate truth.

The past is the richest of storehouses, and it is accessed in only one way—by memory. The memory of the past is contained in individual minds, in the collective memory we call culture, in tree rings and rock strata and the radioactive background of the stars. Almost all human endeavor is the attempt to mine the past for what we need to survive into the future.

This makes remembering indispensable. But it also makes it pleasurable. It is simply enjoyable—with some painful exceptions—to remember what you have experienced in your life. And in telling a story, you do not simply *identify* an occurrence from the past, you live it once more. The mind is able to put you again in that time and place, to re-create the perceptions and emotions, to have "it all come back." It was in your mind that you processed the entire experience in the first place. And it is in your mind that you can have the experience again.

And so the pleasure of remembering is a simple yet profound reason to tell your stories.

Better Understanding Your Own Life and Its Significance

While telling our stories gives us pleasure, it also gives us understanding. Many times, reflecting on a story yields a new and deeper comprehension than we had when it happened. Looking back, with the benefit of more mature minds and subsequent experiences and space for reflection, we can see meanings and patterns and consequences that were hidden from us at the time.

This can be true of any single story and even more true when we start to examine many of them. We discern recurrences and relationships and start making links between things. We may see a plot in our lives, which once appeared random. Our stories may reveal things we like or don't like about ourselves and our lives. Both discoveries are valuable.

The Blessing of Giving to the Giver

It seems a law of the moral universe: being a blessing makes you feel blessed. When others' lives are better because of you, your own life feels richer. It is greatly satisfying to have someone express gratitude for something from your spiritual legacy that they receive as part of their own. You have shown them grace—giving them a gift for which they have not worked—and you feel the grace of it in your own life.

What do I have to give to people I care about and love? I can give them material things (which are decaying even as I give them), I can give them time (which is a great but passing gift), or I can give them the values and insights and guidance that we call wisdom (and which can stay with them forever). In short, I can give them a spiritual legacy, and it starts with stories—the stories of a life lived and reflected on.

The Blessing to the Receiver

The benefits to the giver of a spiritual legacy are profound, but the whole point of a spiritual legacy is to benefit the receiver. We do spiritual legacy work, as opposed to simple memoir or autobiography, because we want to bless someone else's life. That blessing takes many forms.

Most of the benefits for legacy givers are also benefits for legacy receivers. There is, for instance, simple pleasure in sharing in someone else's stories, including people you do not know—hence, our love of novels, films, art, gossip, biographies, documentaries, and everyday conversation ("Anything interesting happen at work today?"). We are designed to process reality through the medium of stories, and we take great pleasure in doing so.

Receivers of stories also benefit from the insights and wisdom those stories transfer. Human progress, even existence, is predicated on our ability to learn from the stories of others. (And failure to learn is the source of much human tragedy and suffering.) This is true for civilizations and for individuals. It is especially true for anyone who receives stories or other spiritual legacy work created directly for them.

When I heard my father's stories, I better understood him, but I also better understood myself. I saw more clearly some of the possibilities and pitfalls of life. His stories helped me steer. Tell your stories to people you love and they will better understand who they are and be better equipped for their own lives. Those who receive story legacies have increased resources for living.

The following is a story told by a man in his eighties, Virgil Olson, that comes from his youth. It contains all of the benefits of a story legacy mentioned above, and is titled, "Sing Just Like Virgil."

Dreams have never had much significance to me. I remember few dreams. However, the messages from a couple of dreams do stand out in my memory. Both were significant in my public life and career.

As a kid I used to dream, more than once, of seeing myself on the platform of a church preaching. There I stood, glaring at the audience. My mouth seemed to be filled with cotton. I couldn't get a word out of my mouth. I felt humiliated, em-barrassed. And when I woke up I vowed I would never become a preacher.

Perhaps the preaching dream repeated itself because my father was a preacher and the members of the church seemed to take it for granted that I was going to grow up and become a preacher, just like my father. But I resented these prophecies. It was not that I did not appreciate and respect my father and his preaching. That was not the problem. At the age of twelve or thirteen I had other goals in life. I was more interested in being a bus driver. I even thought it would be neat to be a conductor on a transcontinental train. That way I could see the country. Those were the days before common commercial air travel.

Other dreams that I had in my youth had to do with singing. I had a pretty good singing voice. When I was in high school I sang in choirs and quartets, and I often sang solos at church services.

One dream I vividly remember. Every time I thought of it I would experience a feeling of tightness, fear. I dreamed I was before a concert audience trying to sing a solo when my voice cracked and I sang off key. People laughed out loud, some got up, making derogatory gestures when walking out of the auditorium. When I awoke from my dream, I was relieved that I was in my small room in my old cast iron bed. I never asked my parents if they heard me howling during the night.

When I was at Bethel Junior College, I did take some voice lessons from Professor George Hultgren, who directed the choirs at Bethel, and who was recognized around the Minnesota music land as a superb tenor soloist.

It was in the fall of 1935. I was a college sophomore. One afternoon after my voice lessons with Hultgren, he told me that he was organizing an all-school choir to present Handel's famous Oratorio, the Messiah. I thought that was great. What a musical challenge. I had never had the opportunity to sing in such a significant and historic musical production.

Then the shocker came. Hultgren said, "Virgil, I want you to sing the tenor solos in the Messiah."

"No," I confusedly replied, "You are the tenor. The presentation of the Messiah without you singing in it would be flat."

"Virgil, you are it," Hultgren said with finality. "I am going to direct the choir. Here, take the book, start working on the first two tenor solos, 'Comfort Ye My People' and 'Every Valley Shall Be Exalted.'"

As I walked out of the room, I had conflicting sensations. I had a dizzying excitement of being asked by George Hultgren to sing the tenor solos in the Messiah. What a challenge. But then I remembered the trauma of my dream. It could all come true.

I will freeze before the people. I will never be able to hit the high notes. My throat will tighten up with a vice grip. I will not be able to do it. And worst of all, the Oratorio begins with these two tenor solos. I will have the first numbers on the program, before any chorus has been sung, before any of the other soloists have had a part. There I will stand, feeling bare naked, trying to get enough breath and voice control to sustain the notes of the opening line in the recitative, "Coooommmfort Ye my people."

I kept taking lessons from Hultgren. He coached me on singing the recitative and aria. And in the meantime, through my teacher's encouragement, I was gaining more confidence.

The evening of the Messiah concert had arrived. It was a Wednesday, about a week before Christmas. The choir members were assembling in the classrooms on the second floor of the college building. (This was on the old Bethel campus on Snelling Avenue, St. Paul.)

Hultgren had imported a guest accompanist and soloists—a soprano, a contralto, and a bass-baritone. I, the tenor, was the only Bethel native to have a solo part.

These soloists were well known in the Twin Cities. They knew each other. They had performed together on several occasions. This evening's performance was only one of two or three Messiah concerts at which they were soloists. They were pros.

Hultgren took me over to this elite circle and introduced me as the tenor soloist. They made perfunctory acknowledgements to me, a young untested tenor sophomore soloist. With a dismissing smile they rattled on in their animated conversation, completely ignoring me.

"Have you seen da da lately? It appears she is putting on some weight."

"I wonder if there is a restroom close by."

"The weather is awful, snow piling up. Hope it lets up by the time we go home."

In the meantime I slowly slinked away. The featured soloists now began to warm up their vocal cords. The bass was belting out the aria, "And I will shaa-aa-ake the nations. The nations!" He sounded awesome. His voice filled the corridors of the second floor.

The soprano, who was a slight woman with a powerful voice, was testing her range. She started at middle G and then threw her voice into high gear to slide up to an octave higher. DoooooEeee. Then up a half step. DooooEeeee—becoming more powerful with each half step on the scale.

The alto was a large, buxom woman who commanded a presence. And she had a voice to match her size. She pulled out all the stops by clearing her vocal pipes, blasting out, holding on to one note with the vowel sounds—eeee, iiiii, aaaaaa, oooooo, uuuuuuu. Then up a note. The same musical voweling.

And I couldn't force out a squeak. My throat was drying up. I felt that my tongue was swelling. I was feeling terribly intimidated. I wanted to get away from it all. Why did I allow myself to be coerced by Hultgren to sing in the Messiah? Didn't he know that I would sound like a bleating lamb beside these confident concertinos?

71

Hultgren was making the rounds, checking on every one, when he saw me in the shadow of one corner of the second floor hallway. He came over and asked me, "Are you okay, Virgil?"

I croaked out, "I'm so scared. I feel so insecure. I keep running to the toilet every few minutes. Why did you choose me to sing this evening?"

"Virgil," he said, "Let me tell you of an experience I had. I was studying voice with a famous teacher in Italy. The time had come for me to give a recital. I felt very insecure singing before an Italian audience. Then my teacher came to me and gave me this word of encouragement."

"George," he said, "There are some who can sing better than George Hultgren. Many who cannot sing as well as George Hultgren. But there is no one in the world who can sing just like George Hultgren. You go out and sing like George Hultgren."

Then Hultgren put his hand on my shoulder. "Virgil. You go out and sing just . . . like . . . Virgil. You will do just fine."

I did. I got through "Comfort Ye" and "Every Valley" with only a slight slip, but I doubt it was noticed by anyone outside the pianist, who covered for me.

However, I have never forgotten the advice. Many times through the years I have been at conferences, special meetings, banquets. And I am one of the speakers among a group of well-known, popular conference preachers.

Then I remember, I have been asked to speak like Virgil Olson. And Virgil Olson is who they will get. Many speak better, of course. Some perhaps not as well. But there is only one Virgil Olson.

I have never forgotten the advice: Go and sing just like Virgil.

This is a story the author clearly takes pleasure in remembering and telling. It helps him better understand and live his life—right to the present day. And it has a clear message that is likely to be a blessing, encouragement, and guide to whomever he chooses to share it.

You have such a story yourself, and someone needs to hear it.

4

Story Legacies

How to Get Started

Stories are the tracks we leave.
Salman Rushdie

It is not difficult to convince most people of the importance of stories. It is often very difficult to convince those same people that they, themselves, are capable of creating a legacy of stories—especially if it involves writing. That is what this chapter is designed to do—move you from "I wish I could write" to "Look what I have written!" It will try to be as straightforward and practical as striking a wooden match: follow these steps and you will end up with a fire.

Story Lists

Simply begin with a list of stories you think worth telling—or at least would like to have preserved for any reason. Everyone has such a list

73

already, because everyone has stories they tell repeatedly, in a variety of situations to a variety of audiences. These are stories we already know how to tell. They have a shape and a rhythm and usually a theme or point—even if the point is just to laugh or to say, "That's how life is." Start by getting those stories down on a list. Write down just enough to remind yourself of the story that needs telling. Just a sentence will suffice.

The best sources for topics are your everyday life experiences—past and present—and your thoughts and feelings about them. Most of what we have learned about life comes from small, not great, events. Meaning and significance in a life build up slowly, like layers around a pearl, from the accumulation of small experiences. Tell the stories of small things and they will grow incrementally into a collective significance that will surprise you—the one who lived it—and delight and bless the ones to whom the stories are given.

After you have listed all the stories that come to you immediately (which may take five minutes or five days), think of the various categories into which we divide life experience and list stories for each of those. These categories are endless—from stories about family, school, and church to stories about friends, work, and travel to stories about firsts, mosts, and bests. If prompts would be helpful, read "Generating Topics" in the appendix.

To give an example of how simple a meaningful story can be, consider the following brief description of the morning ritual of getting up and catching the bus to school during a Minnesota winter, written by Sandy Lind, a woman who grew up in the 1940s. One could say it is only the beginning of a possible story, but it can also stand alone. The author calls it "Catching the Bus."

> The white clapboard-sided, two-story farmhouse stands in the cold, with smoke furling from its chimney. My bedroom window is thickly frosted by Jack Frost. As I begin to awaken, I am aware that my nose is very cold and the rest of me is toasty warm under three heavy bed coverings. The radio in the kitchen, which is just below my bedroom, is on WCCO and the announcer is giving the day's wintry forecast.

I can hear daddy opening the door from the kitchen to the wood shed and then the clang of the stove lid being removed as he adds wood to the fire. A comfortable smell of a waft of smoke and then the aroma of the freshly brewed coffee and delighted sounds of daddy's swallows of that first morning cup of coffee flow up to my bedroom.

Mother has now summoned me for "the final time" to "get up or you'll miss the bus." I move quickly from the covers, placing my feet on the icy-cold linoleum floor. Swiftly I make my way down the winding, steep, narrow stairway into the kitchen. In front of the open oven door I change from my night clothing to my dress for the day.

"Wash your face and comb your hair." The icy-cold orange juice and hot oatmeal, served with fresh cow's milk, were consumed (reminding me for the next four hours of their presence!). Then I put on the boots, heavy slacks (to be removed at school), and heavy coat and mittens. I grabbed my books.

My first breath outside froze. I waited at the end of the driveway, breathing in and out, my nostrils sticking together, watching for the big yellow bus.

There is a lot to be said here about good writing style—note how effectively, for instance, she appeals to all the senses of sight, touch, smell, taste, and sound—but the point I want to focus on is how much significance is caught up in the most ordinary of experiences.

This is in one sense a very objective piece, all description with no overt assertions or reflection of any kind. And yet it exudes values and meaning. There is a subtle sense of belonging and security in this piece (warm bed, hot breakfast). It is significant that this child woke up each morning with a mother cooking breakfast and a father bringing in wood from the shed. There are implied values of responsibility and hard work (cow's milk, school books). There is a subtle affirmation of community values (wash face, comb hair, be on time). Overall, there is an unspoken assertion, one that may be expanded or qualified by other stories, that says, "I was lucky. I grew up well. Life was simple. People loved me. We had what we needed."

At least that's what I see in this very brief story or start to a story. If the author wants me to see something more, something more complicated or double-edged, she is going to have to tell me more. And I hope she does.

EXERCISE ONE

Begin a story list. Focus, in this list, on events. If it helps, start each item on the list with "The time that . . ." All of us can end that sentence a thousand different ways. The time that I fell off the horse, the time my brother cheated on a test, the time my grandmother spanked me for stealing cookies, the time uncle George got drunk on eggnog, the time my father got fired from his job, the time I won the spelling bee.

Do not worry about whether something deserves to be on the list. If you think of it, write it down. You can decide later whether to ever write about it.

Do not limit yourself to "important" stories. At this point, you may not even be sure what the most important stories of your life are. Maybe you never will be certain. Assume all stories, like all lives, are significant.

After you have gotten at least a dozen stories on your list, put a check by those you have told orally on more than one occasion. If that's true of all of them, then check those you find yourself telling most often.

Then put a star by two or three you might want to consider writing down first.

Many of our stories are linked to a place. Versions of the following exercise are popular among teachers of memoir writing.

EXERCISE TWO

Draw a picture of the home you grew up in. (If you grew up in multiple homes, choose one, or do this exercise for more than one home.) You can make a top-down, blueprint schematic. Or you can do a three-dimensional, roof-off picture. Or both. Or any other visual approach that is helpful.

Label each room (don't forget the garage) and put in some of the furnishings—sofas, televisions, dining room tables, beds, stoves, workbenches, where the dog slept, even photographs or paintings on the wall.

Then choose one room and create a story list just for that room. Perhaps it is the warmest room emotionally—or the coldest. What stories do you associate with that room? Which people? What events happened there? What repeated activities?

If you lived for a long time in one house, think of stories from that room at different ages. If you exhaust the stories that come to mind about one room, move on to another.

Now move outside. Start with the yard, the backyard if you had one. Create a heading, "Stories of the Backyard," and go to work.

Then move out of your yard to the neighborhood. Draw a map of it. Label the houses where different people lived—your best friends, the house where people were always yelling, the house of the crabby old guy, the house you could go to if life wasn't going well in your own. What stories do you associate with each house and the people in it?

Now create a story list from the neighborhood. Where did the kids meet to play? What were the favorite street games? Where in the neighborhood did you once have an adventure or get in trouble? When was the first time you explored outside your own neighborhood? If you didn't have a neighborhood, what did you have instead (a farm, an apartment building, a mountainside)?

You could easily get a few dozen stories just from a single exercise like this. Telling kitchen and dining-room stories alone should occupy most people for months. And this exercise touches on only one area of life.

— *Other Visual Aids* —————————————————————————

There is a wide variety of other visual strategies for creating story lists. These include making a timeline of your life. It may be simply chronological—a horizontal line with hash marks indicating key dates and events. Or it may be a road meandering from the top of a page to the bottom and from side to side, with short written comments and simple drawings or symbols, indicating the periods and passages of your life—youth, education, times of sickness, important relationships, jobs, accomplishments and failures, travel, and so on. Or it may involve some other imaginative strategy for picturing your life.

Such mapping can both be a prompt for stories and be included as part of the stories themselves, if you eventually collect a number of them together.

Some people find diagrams helpful. Norma Olson, a woman in a memoir class I taught, created a spoke-and-wheel diagram of her life. At the hub she put her name. On each spoke she wrote a role or different aspect of her life—educator, wife, administrator, mother/grandmother, researcher, Christian, visionary/leader. Alongside each spoke she listed the personal qualities that the role drew out of her—such as tolerance, self-discipline, spirituality, honesty, thoroughness, visioning, and spontaneity. Such a diagram provides excellent raw material for either a spiritual will or a story legacy, and could be helpfully included in both.

Or consider the common strategy of comparing any complex set of relationships to a tree. Draw your life in terms of roots, trunk, and branches. What are the roots out of which your life grows (values, traditions, persons, and ethnic identity, among others)? Draw each root and label it. What is the main thrust, the trunk, of who you are? Write as many terms on the trunk as seem to apply (faith commitments, defining character traits, and the like). Then draw and label the major branches that come off the trunk (profession, roles, stages of life). Last, draw and label smaller branches that are logically connected to the main branches (specific events, people, memories, and other associations). This can be the beginning of a story tree—or a forest!

Other visual strategies include drawing a picture of yourself at different ages and places in your life—a simple stick figure or something more complex. Perhaps dress the figure in clothes you remember from the time (school or work clothes, a prom dress, favorite pajamas or hats). Draw yourself holding significant objects (a baseball bat, a book, a hammer, a pet). If helpful, put yourself in a significant setting. Draw arrows and label different aspects of the drawing. Then use it to add to your Story List.

— *Using the Senses to Prompt the Written* —————————————

All of the above reminds us that there is a vital link between what we perceive with our senses and what we think in our minds and feel in our emotions. (See "Catching the Bus" earlier in the chapter.) My wife remembers with her nose. She is forever asking me, "What does that smell remind you of?" While I am usually stumped, not least because I often smell nothing at all, she traces a smell to a specific time and place—a London double-decker bus, a walk beside the Irish Sea, the trees in a Colorado forest, the "potion" her father used to make for her to drink when she had a cold.

One could easily generate a list of stories based on smells and sounds and tastes and textures—and on the complex associations one has with each (a newborn's cry, a first taste of liver, the feel of a favorite blanket). Our senses provide our first level of interaction with external reality. And that is why it is important to include all those smells and sounds and other sensory details in the stories themselves.

One exercise that has the potential to wed events, persons, and the senses is to use a photograph as a story prompt. Photographs capture a slice of a life, providing a nexus for memory, reflection, and storytelling.

EXERCISE THREE

Choose a photograph that prompts memories and reflection.

Jot down facts and thoughts about the photograph. Where and when was it taken? What is the event and setting, and how is it significant? Who are the people, if any, in the photograph? What is their relationship to each other—literal and emotional?

Look closely at faces. What emotions are being expressed? What is perhaps being revealed about the inner life of each person? What time of life is it for the people in the photograph—generally and specifically?

Is how people are dressed significant? Are there objects in the photograph that reveal something?

Is there a backstory to the photograph? Does the tone of the photograph reinforce or contradict that backstory? (For instance, a photograph in which everyone is smiling but one of the people is dying of cancer or two of them are bitter competitors.)

Who is taking the photograph? Does that invisible person have a role in the scene?

Make a list of stories that this photograph brings to mind.

Here is a story by a young woman, Melissa Kamp, that takes a photograph as its starting point. She titles it, simply, "Grandpa."

> Gazing at the old, black and white picture in my hand, I see the face of a young man staring back. He is outfitted in a dark U.S. Navy uniform with the sailor hat perched on his shaved head. The man's smoothly shaved face is attractive with its strong, well-formed features. Dark eyebrows hover over his clear, captivating eyes. He has a straight nose, and a half-smile is tugging the corners of his mouth, giving him a very carefree, self-assured look. The man's broad shoulders are leaning slightly forward, and his long arms are crossed casually in from of him and resting on a table. His hands are huge, and their strength is somehow visible. On his left hand he is wearing a wedding band. His whole stance seems to declare, "I know what I'm doing!" The man in the picture looks familiar, yet I know I have never seen him. His life was very distant from mine, yet I know his story well. This man is my grandpa.
>
> His picture brings back so many things that I wished for, and also many things that hurt me to think about. Even though he died only a few years ago, I never had a chance to meet him before he died. When I was younger, Grandpa played the role of a fairy tale character in my imagination. He was the man I would dream about. I could envision myself sitting on his lap and listening to him reading me stories. I would dream that we went for walks together. He would tell me what a nice granddaughter I was.
>
> I knew that he really existed, but since I never met him I had to create an existence to fill his place. My parents only told me enough to keep my curiosity at a minimum. When I asked, "Why don't I have a Grandpa Van?" I was told that after WWII

he came home with his "rights" and his "wrongs" mixed up. Grandma knew that he was wrong, and so Grandpa had to leave. That was when my mom was very little. I couldn't understand this reply, but I knew better than to ask any more questions. I made up my own answers.

Grandpa continued to be a mysterious shadow until the day he died. That day, all the questions that I had whirling through my mind about him came out. Before long they were all answered. I learned that Grandpa had always been a strong-willed person. He was also known for being a rebel, and people said that he always tried to shirk from his responsibilities. When my grandma fell in love with him, her relatives warned her that nothing good could ever come of their relationship.

Grandma wouldn't listen to what they said. She loved him and they were married. Within twelve years their family quickly grew. My mother was the last of their six children. Soon after my mom was born, Grandpa left. He had secretly been seeing another woman for quite some time. Grandma filed for a divorce, and as soon as the divorce was final, Grandpa remarried and moved to California.

In the years that followed, Grandpa and his new wife had a baby girl. Eighteen years later this wife died—she had been ill for a very long time. Grandpa remarried again, only one month after her death, and then he moved to Arkansas. That is where he died. He never contacted his children from his first marriage, and they never knew where to reach him. He supposedly tried to get information about them, but they had all married and moved away from where he last saw them.

Grandpa's own relatives wouldn't give him any information that would help him find his children either. When he died, his sister called my uncle to inform us of his death. My uncle and my mom went to his funeral. They met his wife, and they also met their half-sister. They found out what Grandpa did for a job, what was important to him, and learned about who he was as a person. After my mom returned home, she shared with me about who my grandpa really was.

Hearing the truth about my Grandpa made me very angry. I found out that the man I secretly loved and daydreamed about had caused my mom, my grandma, and my entire family a lot of hurt and pain. I wished that I could see him so that I could scream out all of the frustration I was feeling inside. I wanted to make him hear. I wanted to make him realize what he did to people that I loved, and make him pay for all the suffering he had caused.

But now he was dead. There was no one for me to direct my anger at. I could not release my hate. All that I could do was cry.

It has been some time now since Grandpa died, and I now look at his part in my life from a different perspective than before. I will never understand why he left. I still feel anger for what he did, but somehow I have found that it is possible for me to also love him. Looking at this picture makes me wonder if I am like him in any ways. I can see that we have similar features, but what about personality traits? Thinking about him makes me wish that I had known him. I wonder what it would have been like to have him as a grandpa, a grandpa that I could admire and look up to. A grandpa that would love me back.

His picture bears the title of "Grandpa," but there are no memories to fit that title. He never showed that he cared. His absence from my life has shown me how much I long and crave for close family relationships—a relationship that he didn't provide. In my heart, however, I know that I love him. Otherwise I would not be able to call him Grandpa. Love conquers all things. I love you, Grandpa!

The single biggest advantage of the story list is that it overcomes immediately and forever the single biggest obstacle to writing down life stories: "Where do I start?" You start with the next story on the list, or with any story on it that strikes your fancy at the moment.

The problem of what to write about is solved forever because the list always gets longer. In the act of writing or thinking about one story, you will be reminded of two or three others. And the list will help keep you focused. It allows you not to be sidetracked by all the other stories that could be told. If, when writing about the family vacation, you are reminded of a whole host of stories about your uncle Billy's farm, then simply write on your story list "uncle Billy farm stories" and keep on with the one about the family vacation.

No story is too trivial—or painful—to go on your list. Making the list only means you are preserving the memory of it as a possibility for later telling. If you eventually decide to spend your time on other stories, or if you decide telling this story would do more harm than good (to you or someone else), then you can leave it on the list, untold, forever. But putting it there keeps a door open, allows the story to simmer in your subconscious and make the case for itself as you are busy doing other things.

Most every story is worth telling in that every life story honestly told says at the very least, "This is what my life was like." One hopes it also says, "And this is how I felt about it—then and now." Some storytellers, as we saw with the Indian story in the last chapter, give us only the first and not the second. That's okay. We will take what we can get.

But while every story is worth telling, stories meant to be a legacy to someone else are even more important. These are what I will call *values-soaked stories*. I have argued that most stories involving human beings inescapably radiate values. Human beings are a tangle of oughts and shoulds, evaluations and judgments, contentions and assertions. So it is difficult to tell any story without some implied ought in it. Having said that, we can purpose to tell the stories that give flesh to the kinds of values and virtues we identify for the spiritual will. Do you value generosity? What is a story from your life that incarnates something about generosity? The same question goes for compassion, justice, wisdom, curiosity, imagination, humor, or anything else you think important in life. Again, see the "Values, Virtues, and Valuables" list in the appendix.

Put values-soaked stories on your list, but don't let them intimidate you. A story does not have to be weighty or complicated to be profound. Tell a story about having to get up at five every morning to milk the cows—I mean *every* morning, cow udders not taking off Sundays or holidays—and you cannot help but convey something about responsibility and duty and perseverance, even if you do nothing but describe the procedure.

Just describe what it was like if you wish, but feel free also to ruminate, as a cow does, on the events. To ruminate is to chew the cud, and a lot of good life writing, as mentioned earlier, is chewing the cud—reflecting, analyzing, evaluating, making sense of, pondering. Let the story speak for itself if you wish—as we are told to do when writing fiction—but don't be bashful about providing a commentary either. When people tell their stories—orally or in writing—they have the right to offer an interpretation as well (no extra charge).

A story list can also help you see a pattern in your stories even before you write them. Those patterns may be thematic (lots of stories about overcoming, for instance), or based on a person (repeated stories about a grandmother or about teachers), or chronological (a cluster of stories about the teen years, but few from childhood), or patterns of other kinds. Seeing the patterns may lead you for a time to write down stories that are connected in some way before moving on to write other stories with different kinds of connections. This will also suggest ways you may group stories if you later collect them. Think, for instance, of "Army Days" or "Stories from My Travels."

A story list allows the making of a legacy of stories into a lifelong project. Stories beget stories, and you can add to the legacy as often as you wish. Or not. The list is simply an aid, not a taskmaster. When you've told enough stories for the time being, put it away. But not too far away, because you will find yourself often thinking, "That's a story I need to add to my list."

Character Lists

For better or worse, human beings are interested in nothing so much as themselves and other human beings. Even our interest in God, if we have one, is largely about how the nature and existence of God affects *us*. We are speciesist by nature, or by God's design, and all the finger wagging against it won't change the fact. Even stories with only animals as characters are really stories about human beings and human experience.

Therefore, the majority of stories, and a great majority of values-soaked stories, revolve around character and characters. Events are significant, but the reason they are significant is that they involve characters, including you and me. This is helpful to understand when it comes to creating a story legacy because it gives us another strategy for deciding which stories to tell.

We are interested in human beings generally, but we are, more specifically, interested in human nature—in what makes people tick. We will watch a movie about an asteroid threatening to strike the earth and wipe out human life. But we will pay even more attention if the prospect prompts the woman scientist to consider leaving her devoted but boring husband to spend the last three days of earth's existence with a man she's long hankered after.

The British novelist E. M. Forster distinguishes mere events from events involving human nature when talking about what attracts us to story. "The king died, then the queen died" is, he says, simple chronology. "The king died, then the queen died *of grief*" gets us to human nature, the heart of story.

More specifically still, we are most interested in human beings (and human nature) when they are in trouble. We are drawn to stories of people in tough situations, having to make difficult decisions, with something significant at stake. It's not as much fun hearing about someone's struggle to survive if it's guaranteed in advance that they will. Similarly, if a woman is choosing between a man she loves and her career, we are all ears; if she is choosing between driving her Porsche today or driving her Rolls, our attention is likely to wander.

Consider the following story by Elsie Vollman, written in the form of a letter to her adult children:

> We're sitting in a beautiful north woods setting with a gray winter sky looming overhead. As Dad and I were walking earlier this morning, we remembered another winter day several years ago.
>
> It was one of those twenty degrees below zero evenings and we were scurrying homeward from a Bible class at church, over huge banks of hard crusted snow, our arms loaded with Bibles,

folders, and notebooks. The going was precarious, as the side-walks had slippery spots everywhere.

As I was blinking away the tears from the icy wind, I noticed an object on the sidewalk ahead of us. We approached with caution and found it to be a person! Upon closer inspection it was a rotund, old man with a corncob pipe clenched in his teeth, smoke curling around his head.

"Hi there—are you okay?" was all I could muster.

"Yea" he said. "I just fell down and can't get up. Just give me a hand."

After determining that there appeared to be no obvious injury, we decided to attempt a rescue by ourselves. With Dad on one side and me on the other we got a firm grip under each arm and gave a boost. Up he came, quite able to stand for the moment.

"Could you just get me to my house?" he asked. "I live just over there." "Over there" was two doors down the block and it seemed likely we could manage that.

There was no letting go of the old gent as he really couldn't hold his own in the snow and ice and wind. We held firm with one hand, while balancing our books with the other. The narrowly shoveled path toward which he nodded necessitated a "side step" in concert for the three of us. It seemed we'd be able to manage just fine, when he suddenly seemed unable to shuffle further.

Dad groaned a barely audible "Oh no!" He dropped his books and reached downward. The old gent's pants were fall-ing down around his ankles and there he stood in his long underwear!

We glanced at one another and became completely hysterical. It was the funniest sight imaginable! Choking back our laugh-ter, maintaining the underarm hold and tugging at the pants was almost too much to cope with in our weakened condition.

He seemed oblivious to our plight and told us, through clenched teeth of course—the pipe still intact—that he was ninety-three years old and lived alone "since the old lady died." He'd just gone for some evening air and lost his footing.

We did get him into his house, took off his jacket, wrapped him in a blanket, and made him comfortable in his easy chair.

He refused all offers to call a family member to help him,
and assured us he was just fine and "goodnight."

This is a story that has an event, of course, but its significance centers on character and on human nature. In a few paragraphs it gives us a wonderful, values-rich character study of a single human being. Having fallen on the ice, the old man patiently waits for rescuers to come along, still puffing his pipe as though this is just a momentary inconvenience. He is unembarrassed to ask for help, perhaps a little proud of being ninety-three and out for a winter walk, yet determined not to have his independence compromised any more than necessary, certainly not by a call to his family.

The woman who wrote this story, herself well beyond retirement age, wrote it to share with her children. She thought they would enjoy a story—very simply but effectively told, by the way—about their experience with this colorful old man. That was reason enough to tell the story. But it wasn't the only reason.

This story is not only a character study of the old man, but it is also a story about the character of the couple that helped. It tells the children receiving it something about the virtues of their parents. They were the kind of people who went to Bible study in subzero weather, the kind to help someone who needed it, the kind of people who could laugh at a situation while respecting the person in the situation. This is a fine story for a story legacy.

EXERCISE FOUR

A. Make a character list. List significant or interesting people who have been part of your life. You might include someone you have known all your life, or someone you only met once. Because the list will quickly become too long, limit yourself initially to a dozen people. Spread them out among family, friends, schoolmates, coworkers, teachers, and others. They don't have to be the most important twelve, perhaps just the first twelve that come to mind.

B. Pick one person from the list and do a character analysis. Include the following:

—physical: what does the person look like (at a given age)?

—personality: what is their temperament, their personality traits?

—character/values: what was important to them? How did they live their life?

—impact on you: how are you different because of them? What did they teach you?

C. Create a list of stories associated with that one person. Don't worry about whether it is an important story or not. At this point, you are simply generating possible stories to tell.

When you run out of story ideas for one person, move on to the next and repeat the exercise.

D. Choose one story and write it.

Values or Insights List

We talked about values at length in the chapter on spiritual wills. Review that discussion in preparation for a list of stories based on values that are important to you.

Values-rich stories can begin with the story or they can begin with the value. In the first case, one tells a story that for any reason seems worth telling and then either lets the values be implied by the story without comment (as in the description of catching the bus above) or spends time reflecting on what the story might teach or what values it might embody (as in the story about the young African woman with AIDS in chap. 3). You remember something from the past or present, and then in the telling of it you begin to better understand its significance for you and, one hopes, for someone else.

But it is also acceptable to start first with a value or quality or insight and then look for a story from your life that conveys it. I once was trying, for instance, to answer my then-young son's question about whether he had to be nice to a kid at school that everyone else made fun of. I knew the answer was yes, but I also knew that an abstract yes to a real-world question was not likely to be helpful to a young boy. It took me a while, but eventually I wrote him a story. It was the story of when I was twelve and my teacher told me I should ask a disabled girl to dance. (See this and other stories in my book *Letters to My Children: A Father Passes on His Values*.)

I had not thought of that event since it happened, decades before. But when I started thinking about my son's predicament—burdened with a moral system that told him he should be kind to unpopular kids—that experience popped into my mind and I wrote a "Dear Matthew" letter to him that told the story. It has since become a very important story for me and, I hope, for him.

EXERCISE FIVE

Look again, or for the first time, at the exercises in the "Spiritual Will" chapter.

Make a list of values or insights about life that are important to you. If you think, for instance, that people are more important than possessions, start with that conviction.

Then begin a list of stories from your life that demonstrate that truth. Do the same with other values.

Intersecting Lists

If you follow the suggestions above, you will have three lists—a story list focusing on events; a character list focusing on people; and a values list focusing on values, virtues, and insights. Any one of them can provide a great number of stories worth telling. If you want to tell your most powerful stories, however, look for where the lists intersect.

Our most important stories are likely to involve an important character engaged in an important event, which together embody an important value or life lesson. Therefore, look at your three lists and see where they overlap. When a character from your character list is part of an event from your story list that suggests a value from your value list, *that* is a story you need to tell. That is a story that is part of your spiritual legacy. You need to preserve it—for your own good and for someone else's.

Here is such a story, written by a young man in his twenties, Jeremy Huggins, demonstrating yet again that spiritual legacy work is not just for those on the backstretch of life.

On Saturday mornings, the children would wander through the Brookville Gardens Project, congregate on my stoop, and wait. I wanted to make them long for, talk about, wonder what happened inside 11-C before granting them entrance to my home—ritual is good for the children. But ritual could never compete with the ebony symphony of giggle outside my sheet-metal door, so I'd give, and they would flood my home. I like to think they came because they liked me, their white Moses. Maybe so. But I know that they came because they liked the silly man whose kitchen poured forth chips and pop, a river of energy: mighty, eternal. It was my peace offering: a taste of reconciliation, I hoped.

When they'd finish the chips, I would feed them Bible stories, after which they would offer up prayers for granmamas and no more fighting in the world, amen, burp competitively, giggle, and leave. And 11-C was my sanctuary again—curtains fingered with grease, pop puddled on the linoleum. But I didn't mind. It was their ritual, their benediction to me.

After restoring cleanliness and order, I would entertain my own ritual: sit in my rocking chair and quietly eat a banana. It was not glorious, but it was my own. And, usually, it was all that was left unmangled—one holy bunch of bananas on top of the refrigerator.

On one of those Saturdays, soon after the children returned home, and during the last bite of banana, my door rattled (it would rattle at the slightest breeze until I opened it and re-jammed a wad of napkin in the top-left corner.) Only at this opening, it was not the breeze—it was Lamarcus, a four-foot-three bundle of Africa in my doorway.

"Lamarcus, hey, man, what up?" (Maybe he didn't get a pop earlier; the bigger kids were not afraid to cash in on their bigness.)

"Chillin'. Chillin'," he said.

"Chillin'? You wanna come in?"

"A'ight."

He stepped in, and I squatted eye-level with him and scrunched my nose, thinking maybe that he had come for the Bible I'd promised the kids that morning, preparing to tell him that he needed to wait until next week for that, and I would see him then.

Lamarcus hadn't come for the Bible. Lamarcus came for the kitchen. At least that's where he went. So I went back to the den, sat slowly, exhaled audibly, and practiced smiling, pretending to be glad for his presence. During the third smile, he came in, sat—hands empty, lips slightly closed—and fixed his eyes somewhere between the brown-shagged floor and my chin.

"So, Lamarcus . . . what's up?" Maybe he just needed a little prodding. Some prodding is good for the children.

"Nuttin'."

And I found my eyes fixing themselves somewhere between the browns of the floor and his eyes. And we sat in silence for seven minutes, like ghetto monks observing the rule.

Then they changed—his eyes, they turned down like the peel in my hand, brows curved in supplication. He had begun rocking to some ancient rhythm, planted in him, I might have imagined, by some ancient seed. But I was just annoyed by the movements. And by the eyes that I didn't understand as they turned to my banana.

Then he broke the silence.

"You know . . . sometimes . . . people be sayin' I like bananas."

"Lamarcus, do you want a banana?"

"Ooh, you got some bananas?"

Lamarcus. Beautiful, seven-year-old, four-foot-three Lamarcus. How you mortified your desires then so that I could rest seven more minutes. Such sacrifice for a child. How you became my friend as we peeled bananas together.

Lamarcus stopped coming with the rest of the kids. He began coming on his own, sometimes at 6:00 in the morning, waiting for the bus; sometimes late at night, wearing a ski mask, hoping

91

to scare the white man in the project. But faithfully he came, often just to sit, always to eat our bananas. One time he came for his promised Bible. A rattle at the door.

"Lamarcus. What's up, man?"

"Chillin'. I could have my Bible now?"

"Yeah, Lamarcus. Come on in for a few minutes."

He sat and fingered the pages of his Bible as if the black-and-white of it were alive. Then he raised his eyes to meet mine, and his lips split like the Red Sea as he pronounced his benediction: "Tight. Dat's tight."

You know . . . sometimes . . . people be sayin' I like Lamarcus. I loved him, and I love him: Lamarcus of the ashen skin and sacrificial heart.

That was years ago. I moved far away, now living at the other end of a long, dull highway, grey and worn like sheet metal. Too far for visits. So I sit in my rocking chair and imagine what he looks like now. I miss him. But one day soon, I'll look over Jordan and see him—glorious, skin burnished bright black, asking Jesus for a banana.

This is a story that could have arisen from any number of places. It could have been prompted by the memory of an event, or a desire to show the strange ways of love, or, perhaps most likely in this case, the wish to celebrate a little boy that once crossed the writer's path. But because it has all three—event, character, and value—it is an important story for the writer that we are the better for having heard.

Moving from *Which* to *How*

We have addressed how to find a story to write about, but not how to actually get one written. For every person who laments, "I don't know what to write about" there are fifty who say, "I don't know how to write it." Some of the obstacles are psychological and others are practical, structural, or strategic. I will briefly address the psychological and practical ones first and offer specific advice on writing in a later chapter.

Psychological Barriers

The single biggest fear of writing is the blank page (or blinking cursor on an empty screen). To help you deal with this situation, there are endless books on writing that offer tips for overcoming writer's block, finding inspiration, and building self-esteem. Read them if you think they'd be helpful.

If you don't have time, consider the following tips:

—Do not (I repeat, do not) say to yourself, or to anyone else, "I am going to write my life story." That is the absolute quickest way to paralysis and to turning on the television instead of writing something down. And it isn't true. A story legacy is not an autobiography. Tell yourself instead, "I am going to write down one story. It may be the only story I ever write down. It may be only a page long. For now, I will just think about this one story and this first page. Whenever I finish this story, if I ever do, I might write down another one someday. Or I might go to a movie. But for now, I am going to work on this one story."

—Do not worry about how the story should begin. You don't have to start at the beginning. In fact there are advantages to not starting with the beginning. Start wherever your memory and imagination tell you to start. If later you decide the reader needs more information earlier, then add more at that time. But start anywhere you want and let the beginning and the ending take care of themselves.

—Do not worry about the words. You have started almost every sentence you have ever spoken in your life without knowing what words you were going to use or how the sentence was going to end (just as I did in writing this sentence). Your brain is full of words, and it will provide them when needed. Don't stop to insist on better words from your brain. Just use the words that come at the moment. You can tinker with it later.

—If you feel the need to put your toe in the water first, start with a favorite story you have told orally many times. You already know how to tell that story. You know where it starts and how it ends and what happens in the middle. Just transcribe your inner voice telling it again. (Or have someone else transcribe it.) You may find that a written story needs a few things that an oral story doesn't, but those are details to worry about later.

—Tell your inner critic to go fly a kite. That voice that says, "You can't do this," "You're not a writer," "No one wants to hear your stories," "Wait and do this later," is the same voice that tells you you're too fat or skinny, that your sibling is having a better life than you are, that God is really, really upset with you, and that your favorite baseball team will never win the pennant. Okay, so now I'm sounding like a cheerleader from those writing books, but you get the idea. Maybe you should say to your inner critic, "You're right. I am a lousy writer. But there's someone who needs this story, and I'm going to write it anyway. So get lost."

—Ask yourself this: If *you* could have an important story from someone you loved, would you complain about the wording?

Creating the Time to Write

I do not accept the excuse from people who claim they would like to write but they do not have the time to do so. If we value something enough, we find the time to do it. Not finding the time tells us that we value it less than much else for which we do manage to find the time. The proof of valuing is in the finding. If you haven't written anything yet, it is because you found other things to do that seemed to you more important.

Having said that, here are tips for increasing your chances of actually getting something written.

The first is that you do not find time; you *create* it. Hoping to find time is like hoping to win the lottery. We don't *find* money; we *make* money. We also make time for whatever is important to us.

The best way to create time for telling your stories is to *schedule* it rather than wait for it. Take out your calendar. Make *writing appointments* with yourself. Then defend those appointments against competing claims the same way you would defend a doctor's appointment or a meeting with a friend. Choose the times wisely. If the weekends are the only time you could realistically do spiritual legacy work, then block out your Saturday mornings. If every Saturday morning is unrealistic, then block out two Saturday mornings a month. If the entire morning is unrealistic, then block out eight to ten. But once you've blocked it out, don't let something else push it aside. You say a spiritual legacy is important to you, so prove it by giving it time to happen.

Second, do not assume that good writing requires extended chunks of time. That is the ideal, but life often gets in the way of the ideal. Use even fifteen- and twenty-minute opportunities. These can be especially good times for making story or character lists, or for brainstorming, or for editing something you've already written, or for jotting down ideas.

Third, try to end each writing session with a sentence or topic that you can begin with the next time you write. We waste a lot of time starting things, especially if much time has passed since we last worked on something. If we spend the last few minutes of a writing session putting down thoughts or sentences that we can reread and start with when we come again, we will more quickly get up to speed in the new session.

If it is helpful, take a class, or join or create a writing group. Some people find they are more successful when accountable to others, even strangers. Make sure the group genuinely focuses on writing, not on talking about how nice it would be to write. (People reading their stories to others counts as writing.)

Whether writing alone or with others, a writing schedule exploits the amazing cumulative effects of small but repeated efforts. Five pages a month yields sixty pages a year, and a decade of such efforts yields six hundred pages of your spiritual legacy. Do you have ten years or more to live? Then get going. If not, then get going even sooner.

5

Telling Your Master Stories

To belong, to be witnessed, to be remembered, to have your life make a difference, to bless and be blessed—all have a place in your legacy.

Rachael Freed

Every story has value, because every story preserves some aspect of the human experience. We need them all. But some stories are more defining than others. Some are more enduring, more shaping, more explanatory, more revealing, more inescapable. I call these master stories. Everyone has them, and the more aware we are of how they operate in our lives the better. Some of these master stories need to be told to others.

I got the term "master story" from Michael Goldberg, a Jewish theologian who argues that Judaism and Christianity center on two different central narratives, found in the two testaments of the Bible, that define each (see *Jews and Christians: Getting our Stories Straight*). The master story for Judaism, he says, is the exodus story. God rescues the people of Israel from their four-hundred-year oppression in Egypt,

97

names them as his people and himself as their God, and leads them to the promised land.

Israel thereafter defines itself as the people whom God rescued out of Egypt. It is a constant refrain throughout the Hebrew Bible. Whenever Israel wanders from this story, someone—a prophet, king, warrior, judge, or other leader—rises up to remind them that this is their master story, the one that tells them who they are.

For Christians, Goldberg argues, the master story is the Easter narrative. God has become Emmanuel, one with us, sharing the human experience in the person of Jesus the Messiah. He died for our sins, was buried and resurrected, then ascended into heaven, from whence he shall come to judge the quick and the dead. The fact that my mind and typing fingers went to a creedal formulation (leaving out a few parts) is instructive. The church historically turned its foundational teachings into creeds, which usually are a condensed story line. When we stand together and recite a creed, we are announcing our commitment to a common story, the story that tells us who we are and what we are to do.

A Definition of Master Story

My street-level definition of a master story is as follows: *a master story is one of a handful of stories that explain your life to you and tell you how to live.* Both its explanatory and its directive power are crucial. Master stories do not merely entertain, or capture some experience, or pass along some ideas or values; they claim to illuminate life, to tell us how things are, to make connections. They do at a macro level (sometimes called *metanarratives*) what every story does at a micro level. Little stories would like to grow up to be big ones.

Characteristics of Master Stories

Master stories have certain features:

A master story is one that helps explain your experience to you. We do not simply remember stories; we think and feel with our stories. If I have been the victim of racial persecution, the story of that persecution will explain to me how the world works. It will explain to me why the officer stopped my car even though I was not speeding, or why the rental property I am inquiring about is suddenly unavailable. If I am a person of faith, *that* master story will explain why the world is so messed up and what should be done about it.

A master story embodies and crystallizes your values. It is perhaps a chicken-and-egg matter as to whether we are drawn to certain master stories because they embody the values we already hold, or whether our master stories tell us what is important to begin with. Clearly both are at work. But either way, our master stories include what is most important to us or they would not be master stories. I am drawn to God in part because God cares about justice, and, at the same time, I learn from God what true justice is and value it even more highly.

A master story helps you make decisions. It does so by offering a standard against which to make judgments. If the gospel story of the woman caught in adultery is a master story within *the* master story for me—and it is—I will use it when I find myself confronted with similar dilemmas. The story shows Jesus asserting the proper balance between compassion ("Neither do I condemn you") and affirming a moral order ("Go and sin no more"). Living as I do in a world both relativistic and intolerant, that master story gives me help in finding a path between two unhealthy extremes.

A master story is one you return to in times of trouble, pain, or confusion. When life turns bad—for individuals or for communities—we return to our master stories. They both console and reorient us. They console us because they have big answers for big problems, giving us the comfort of explaining the pain and confusion we feel. They also are familiar, and the familiar is comforting when we suffer. Sometimes they are consoling because the cause of the pain or trouble is that we have wandered away from the master story, and the return is a coming home. And they reorient us by reminding us of the direction of true north: what is important, what is meaningful, who cares about us, and what it all means in the end.

A master story is one that you are willing to take risks for. We will take risks for our master stories because all of the characteristics mentioned

99

above make them unusually valuable, even indispensible. If you are not willing to take chances for a story in which you are a character, it is not a master story for you.

Not every master story will have all of these characteristics, but the most important ones will.

Categories of Master Stories

Master stories come in all shapes, sizes, and categories. Here are some:

Political

Politics, like so much else, is all about stories. An election is essentially a battle of stories, each side trying to convince the electorate that they have the better one. There are many large political master stories in the world: conservatism, liberalism, socialism, libertarianism, authoritarianism, to name a few. Each repeats smaller master stories that inform and energize it. American liberals like to tell stories of Joe McCarthy's 1950s red-baiting because it identifies an enemy and energizes its followers even many decades later; conservatives are equally eager to rehearse the story of Neville Chamberlain's naive appeasement of Hitler because they believe it tells them what to do in the present world.

Ideological

There is overlap between the ideological and the political, but large ideological master stories include feminism, environmentalism, Marxism, capitalism, multiculturalism, and the like. Each of these tells the stories that define it and inspire its followers. When ideological master stories conflict with each other, the battle is more often carried out with stories than with bombs.

Historical

Sometimes the key to understanding someone is understanding the defining historical events they experienced, especially in their formative years. As a boy, I didn't understand why my grandparents thought a fifty-cent tip in a restaurant was adequate until I learned about the Depression. You won't understand Israeli politics unless you understand something about the Holocaust and the expression *never again*, nor George Bush's foreign policy decisions until you explore the effects on him of standing in the ruins of the World Trade Center. Understanding someone's master stories does not require affirming their narratives, but the way to begin to know someone is to understand the stories that shape them.

Religious

No stories are more powerful than religious ones, because none are so ambitious. Religion seeks to explain not just this life but eternity as well. It has something to say about most everything. It is intensely personal and pervasively public at the same time, no matter how much some people try to restrict it to the private sphere. And it is unapologetically filled with oughts and shoulds. Religion attracts us because it promises so much, and that is why it is dangerous when it fails.

Personal

Some of my master stories are shared with millions, others with a few, some are known only to God and me. At times a single event can be the shaping story of an entire life: a success or failure, abuse, a divorce, some great friendship, the death of a loved one, a car wreck, a transforming spiritual experience. These stories reside in our bones, shaping in often unrealized ways our entire conception of life. Many of these will arise from family. I wondered for years about the particular passions and emphases of a pastor I respect; then I heard him talk about his father on one occasion, and many of my questions were answered. This sudden insight was not the product of pop psychology; it came from a glimpse of one of his personal master stories.

Each of us has a unique constellation of master stories. We will defend them even when they seem irrational or toxic to others, because they are *our* stories and they work for us and we do not trust the alternatives.

Which is why any genuine conversion—political, relational, religious, or otherwise—is so difficult. Ask someone to become a Republican instead of a Democrat, a free-market capitalist instead of a socialist, a Christian instead of a secularist, and you are asking them to change their master stories, something they are unlikely to do unless the old ones no longer work for them and the new ones are powerfully attractive.

The difference between most stories and a master story is the directive nature of the latter. We tell many useful stories that do not, in themselves, tell us how to live. They are often revelatory, but they are not necessarily ordering and insistent in the way a master story often is.

The Pros and Cons of Master Stories

Master stories are always formative, but they are not always healthy. We cannot live well without them, but sometimes we cannot live well with them either, depending on how they work in our lives. We need, therefore, to understand more about them. Consider the following:

All of us have master stories, whether we have identified them or not. Even those who think metanarratives (large-scale explanations of reality) oppressive, do so because of their own metanarrative. Human beings are storytelling creatures, and some set of stories or another will always rise to the level of master stories for each one of us. This is a good thing, because without master stories we get no Gandhi, no Martin Luther King Jr., no Sojourner Truth, no Rachael Carlson, no Aleksandr Solzhenitsyn, no movements for justice, no shared values.

At the same time, *master stories can be healthy or unhealthy.* All stories are not created equal. Some master stories are false. They tell us lies—about the world and about ourselves. Tell a child she was an "accident" or not a favorite of her grandmother and you may have unwittingly created a master story that will echo for decades. Nazism was a master story. So is the story of consumerism and materialism, the story advertising tells us over and over.

Healthy stories have certain qualities. Such stories are, among many other things, freeing, grace-filled, nurturing, truthful, and filled with reasons for living. (For more, see my book *Tell Me a Story: The Life-Shaping*

Power of Our Stories.) We do well to assess the health of our master stories and abandon the toxic ones, as difficult as that may prove.

One reason for this difficulty is that *master stories serve as gate-keepers.* Master stories determine not only what we believe is true and important in the world, but they also determine what we allow as evidence in making that determination. Master stories tend only to allow evidence that confirms the story. They are both self-verifying and self-perpetuating. If, on the one hand, you believe in angels, you will find evidence for angels. If your master story says there is nothing in the universe beyond the material world, Gabriel himself could appear at the foot of your bed and you will simply ask yourself, "What was on that pizza, anyway?" Evidence is only evidence if it is allowed to be evidence.

Many of the tensions and tragedies in the world are, at the most fundamental level, story collisions. Catholic versus Protestant in Northern Ireland, Jew versus Palestinian, Islam versus the West, liberal versus conservative, husband versus wife, parent versus child, friend versus friend—in all these cases the antagonists each have their stories. Story collides with story, partial truth collides with partial truth, and the damage is incalculable.

But there is hope. *Master stories can be restored, modified, or replaced.* Neither individuals nor communities need be trapped forever in destructive stories. Sometimes we need to restore a master story to its original healthy state. Distorted political or religious or personal stories can be healed. Other times we need to modify our story. In extreme cases, a sick master story needs to be entirely replaced. Sometimes when two stories collide, whether within a family or between nations, we must seek a third story in which all sides can envision themselves living. Reconciliation requires the healing of stories.

Examples of Master Stories

A Story within a Master Story

Turn back to the poem that opened the first chapter and read it again, along with my comments. This poem shows how a master story can arise from more than one category, here both historical (the Depression) and personal (an outing with her father). Is this a master story for Marilyn Boe? I don't know for certain, but it has all of the elements.

It helps her understand the world—then and now. It embodies her father's values and insights and shows him trying to pass them on to her for her good. It is a story the writer can use to make difficult present-day decisions in time of trouble, pain, or confusion. The values implied in the poem are ones that she likely is willing to take risks in order to defend. And by telling the story, she is making this master story a part of her spiritual legacy for the benefit of others.

A Playground Bully

Here is another story, this one from a middle-aged woman named Stephanie Cunningham. She calls her story, "When I Hit Bruce in the Head with a Rock."

> On the playground, as the students parted like the Red Sea, across the way Bruce appeared before me like Charlton Heston in *The Ten Commandments*. As he began his daily ritual, I reached down to pick up a rock. Today would be different.
>
> I always felt I wasn't the same as the other kids. I just had a slight problem with walking. Some of them constantly rocked back and forth in their chairs all day, never speaking. Many used wheelchairs because their legs didn't work right. Others drooled and their limbs spasmed as they tried to talk. A few had no arms or legs at all. I knew I didn't belong in this place. I desperately prayed to go to the "normal" school my older brother and sister attended. I just wanted to be like everybody else.
>
> My prayers were answered when, as a world-weary fourth-grader, I moved to Our Lady of Victory Catholic grade school. We all dressed alike in our crisp white blouses, blue and red plaid uniforms with dark blue cotton sweaters. To this school look, I added twenty pounds of steel long-legged leather braces and occasionally used stick crutches. It was 1968.

The first months after arriving were difficult and scary. The nuns would stop and tell me they were praying for me every day. Their pity could be felt in every glance. Most of the students seemed leery of me. They had never met someone who was disabled, let alone someone their age and disabled. Many ignored or left me alone; a few befriended me. A small number decided to torment me.

The worst was a boy named Bruce. I remember him so clearly. He had a short crew cut and though he dressed like the other boys—dark blue pants, white shirt and black shoes—he stood out from the crowd because he had a nice face.

Week after week I put up with his constant name calling and teasing. Adding insult to injury, he would dance circles around me. He started early as we were all unloading from the school buses. Then, he'd track me down during morning and afternoon recesses. Sometimes he would gather a friend or two to join him during the lunch hour. With his handsome features contorted in a devilish grin, he'd screamed in my face, "Hey iron legs, is Frankenstein your daddy?" Or, "Retard, retard, spazzing in the schoolyard." The other kids would giggle, quietly watch or pretend nothing was happening.

At first, I tried to ignore him. Then I began yelling back. Finally I tried hitting him, but I could never make contact. He'd quickly back away just far enough so that I couldn't reach him. With a self-satisfied grin, he would keep taunting me and then swagger away.

One sunny spring day, as the recess bell rang, everyone started towards the school doors. Since I had difficulty climbing the three flights of stairs, I was allowed an extra ten minutes to get from class to class. Bruce hung around, sitting across the playground from me. As he watched me make my way to the building, he began his usual taunts. I yelled at him to stop. He didn't.

Something happened to me that day. Staring at him for a second and without even thinking, I picked up a rock the size of a handball. My upper body was very strong from years of using crutches and maneuvering up and down the staircase to my bedroom, not to mention pushing myself in wheelchairs around the hospital after numerous surgeries. I had biceps to die for. I also had a very keen eye.

Bam!

The next thing I knew, Bruce was on his back, crying. I had hurled the rock at him. I immediately headed into school, terrified. I may have experienced a miracle that day: I ran, I actually ran, praying over and over again "Jesus, Mary, and Joseph, please help me!"

Finally arriving at my classroom I plopped down at my desk, still frantically chanting to the holy trio. Suddenly the classroom phone rang. After taking the call, Sister Dymphna turned towards the class and looked straight at me. "Stephanie, the Principal wants to see you. Now!"

Slowly I made my way to Sister Fabian's office. As I stepped into the room, I saw Sister, the school nurse and Bruce. The nurse was taping a large gauze band-aid over Bruce's right eye. Sister said, "Stephanie, Bruce says that you hit him in the eye when you were coming back to class after recess. Is that true?" Looking up at Sister, then over to Bruce, then back at Sister, I tried to think of something brilliant to say to get out this mess.

Shaking my head with as much wide-eyed innocence as I could muster I said, "Oh nooo Sister, I would never do something like that. I know what it's like to be hurt and in pain." Bruce lunged at me, screaming "Liar!" The nurse struggled to hold him back. Sister glared at Bruce and turned to me with a knowing smile. "I didn't think so child. You can go back to class." Bruce continued yelling as I quickly closed the door and began my new heart-felt prayer of thanks to Jesus, Mary, and Joseph.

Bruce was not seriously injured and his eyesight returned to normal. At the end of that school year, he and his family moved across country when his father received a job promotion. It would be eleven years before I saw Bruce again.

In a crowded local burger joint on a first date, John and I were sitting in a booth, chatting and waiting for our food. All of a sudden, out of the mass of people in the bar, Bruce appeared. With no introduction, no hello, he slammed his hands down on our table and growled, "How could you lie to a nun? How could you?" I knew it was Bruce—there was that face! And even though he didn't wear a crew cut any longer, he looked exactly the same, just a little bit taller and older.

Stunned, I slowly replied, "Wow. . . Bruce? How are you?" He didn't answer. He just glared at me shaking his head. Looking at him I thought, how remarkable! That after all these years, it was me lying to a nun, that was all he recalled. Incredulous, I shook my head. "Are you kidding me? Really Bruce—that's all you remember? Not any of your taunting and teasing, for months on end?" I continued, "What do you think your ridiculing did to me; how it made me feel?"

Bruce was now gazing at me without speaking for the longest time. As his stormy face softened, it took on a subtle but stunned expression. It was clear he had never thought about it from that perspective. He had never thought about my feelings or his behavior at all. Looking me squarely in the eye, he whispered, "My God! I . . . I'm sorry." With that, he turned and disappeared into the crowd.

Here is a story about pain, perseverance, cruelty, revenge, poetic justice, and ethical confusion. It seems to be a life marker for the writer, a story that embodies many different elements of her childhood— disability, desire for normality, unkindness, overcoming, and more. It has the complexity and ambiguity of real life, a likely candidate for a master story.

Identifying Your Own Master Stories

Only you have your particular configuration of master stories, and only you can tell them. Here are some exercises designed to help you identify what some of them might be. Do not expend much effort in deciding whether a particular story from your life is genuinely a "master" story or "just a story." (Sometimes the act of writing will make it clear.) It does not have to be *the* central story of your life, simply one that still moves you and helps you understand your life.

EXERCISE ONE

Look at the description of the various categories of master stories indicated above: political, ideological, historical, religious, personal. Make a story list under each category. What stories, for instance, have gone into shaping your political views? Why, besides abstract ideas, are you a conservative or liberal or something else? What were your family's political leanings, or your friends'? Did a life experience teach you something politically important?

Once you have some lists from a variety of categories, compare them. Do some stories arise in more than one list? Are your ideological commitments shaped by a historical event that had a personal dimension? Do your religious or ideological convictions have a political expression that is captured in a story? Have you, for instance, ever volunteered or marched for a cause, participated in a boycott, organized resistance to something you thought was wrong? Tell the story.

EXERCISE TWO

Reflect on specific individuals who have shaped how you see the world. These can be people you know—family members, friends, teachers—or people you don't know—past or present thinkers, public figures, activists, spiritual leaders, writers or artists or musicians. Their influence on you may or may not be tied to an event. The story of how a book or film changed your life can be a master story. Books and ideas *happen* to us, just as events do, especially if they affect how we subsequently act in the world. (And those books often contained many stories themselves.) Tell the story of how you were changed.

EXERCISE THREE

Some master stories are toxic. They stunt or diminish us or tie us in knots. Identify some of those as well. What are stories—from family, or school, or church, for instance—that have shaped you in harmful ways. Tell some of those stories and how you overcame them—or how you hope to.

These stories, too, are part of your legacy, but they are a legacy whose destructive power you do *not* want to pass on. In a sense, the goal with telling toxic stories is to *lessen* their significance, to turn them from being master stories that still shape us to being "just stories" that document our past but no longer do us harm. The telling of them is sometimes the first step to healing.

But be aware that such stories are potentially dangerous, especially stories of abuse. Some should only be told with the aid of others who can help you get beyond their reach.

Never Too Young to Have a Master Story

We must constantly resist the common notion that legacy work is for old people. It *is* a primary responsibility for the last third of a life of normal length, but it is something that is invaluable at any age. (And no one—young or old—can know how soon their life will end.) I believe the following story, written by a twelve-year-old boy named Hunter Friesen, has some of the markings of a master story. He calls it "Silent Paw Prints."

> I grinned. Despite the bitter, bone-chilling cold, I was thrilled. This was the day I had been looking forward to for months, for what seemed like an eternity. My dad and I were in Ely, Minnesota, for the trip of a lifetime. We were dog mushing. I was awestruck by the open enclosure that was the dog yard and the chorus of howls, barks, whines, and growls that were the dogs.
> "Are you ready, kid?"
> The gruff voice of our guide painfully sliced through my delighted amazement. It angered me slightly to have that moment broken, but he was our guide and whatever he said was important. I answered his question with a silent nod, nothing more. He then proceeded to explain in detail how to carefully unhook the dogs from their chains and lead them back to the truck that would transport them to our trailhead. Leading them was nigh impossible; they were the ones who truly were leading us with their sleek bodies of pure muscle.

The drive to the trail seemed to take hours as the excitement boiled up in my mind.

"How fast will they go? Will I tip over? Will I be dragged off a mile from where we're supposed to be?"

All these questions and more plagued my mind. When we arrived it turned out that we were in store for yet more work. However, harnessing an eager Alaskan Husky is much easier than it sounds. Each husky earnestly lifted a paw (or two) to help me get the harness on so that we could run sooner.

After hooking up the dogs, our guide gave us brief instructions on how to direct a sled team. With the simple command "hike" we were off at an exhilarating speed. To say we hit the ground running is not completely accurate, since I don't recall actually touching the ground.

Despite the pain from the ice shards kicked up by the sled, the rhythmic beating of each silent paw step lulled me into a peaceful trance. I was content with myself. Each whiff of sweet, minty pine scent in the air added to this sacred feeling's allure. The crunch of every paw step felt important, and I gradually forgot everything but The Feeling. The darkness of the pine cover made me drowsy while zipped inside the sled, and I felt like I was one of the dogs, silently running, running silently. Quietly, I hoped for The Feeling never to stop. But alas, all things must stop, even for simple things like lunch.

Though I regretted stopping, I was rather hungry, and the meal was a feast in the snow. From the sweet richness of the hot chocolate to the spiced warmth of the chicken soup, the meal was simple but felt like the best I'd ever had.

"Surely," I thought to myself, "the Iditarod is not as hard as it seems when you are consumed by The Feeling; surely they bear it better than they say." The time for eating and my contemplations was short but seemed long with the anticipation for The Feeling. We packed up. This time I would lead the team, and when I spoke the command I had already given in to The Feeling.

Every sound, smell, and taste was so much clearer on the final half of the trail's loop. I even dared look at my surroundings and found that they were beautiful and tranquil.

And then I noticed something incredibly amazing: even the birds were hushed, as if to submit to the majesty of the dogs. Though the dogs weren't ours it felt as if they were mine to be with and to run with as my friends. The pleasant trance seemed to last forever.

But something this perfect couldn't last—all too soon it was over, was done. I promised to remember The Feeling and all its emotions. My memories would not be like the silent paw prints of the dogs. They would not be brushed away or filled in by a blizzard of other memories.

This is certainly an entertaining and well-written story, but why might it be called a master story? You need to know one more thing about the writer's life. As a child, Hunter was terrified of dogs. He avoided going outside if a dog was in the street. He preferred even a small dog to be held if he was in the room with it. Dogs and fear went hand in hand. Going mushing at the age of twelve with loud, barking, aggressive dogs was the culmination of a long process of overcoming his fear. It was nothing short of an act of bravery.

Now Hunter has his own dog and associates dogs with The Feeling, something that involves much more than the excitement of mushing. It is a Feeling that he will pursue in other contexts for the rest of his life, one that will not be "brushed away . . . by a blizzard of other memories." And that is what potentially makes this a master story.

Master Stories in Process

Master stories do not come only from the past. Some arise today that will shape our tomorrow. Some await us in the future. The following is a master story by Scott Crook, owner of a small hotel in Tegucigalpa, Honduras, written at the time it was happening. It was not created at a writing table during quiet moments of reflection. It was pounded out hastily at a keyboard, through tears, while the rain was still falling. It was sent out as desperate pleas for help in emails to family and friends. (What follows condenses three separate emails.) It needs no title.

111

We are all okay, but large parts of the city have been destroyed. Forty bridges (with clearance of fifty to seventy feet) have been swept away so far. They are rationing food, gas, and electricity. Our hotel is loaded with people who cannot leave. We can't feed them all for long. It is still raining. Looting of stores has begun. Please pray for Honduras. I have never in my life seen such destruction.

We are currently in a State of Emergency. Tegucigalpa looks like an atomic bomb hit it. Only the carcasses of buildings and bridges are left. We know and trust that the Lord has control over everything. We have no idea why a disaster of this magnitude would occur in this already very poor country. Many churches have been holding services, giving out food, and holding vigils.

There are no words to describe what one sees. In the morning I was helping some friends shovel out their house. It was useless, a total loss. In the late morning I helped pull out a friend of the family from his house. He was dead and we couldn't find his wife until about one in the afternoon. One minute you are thanking God nothing happened to you and the next feeling overwhelmed with almost guilt in comparison with what has happened to so many others. What is really hard to understand are the looters. I just cannot comprehend what they are doing.

In the afternoon Eduardo and I went to the Boy Scouts to help bag food. It was an assembly line type of operation. Beans, rice, milk, candles. Most of the stuff was edible—really wet, but hopefully enough to keep some more people alive. Around 4:00 we got the terrible news that our Mayor of Tegucigalpa was killed in a helicopter accident. He was a special type of politician; we really saw a difference with him. Things were really changing; he was probably the next president. His son is a personal friend of ours and he worked in the hotel up to two months ago. It is as if this is a terrible dream and you can't wake up. . . . What is next?

Watching CNN gives you no idea of what is going on. As I write all this to you guys, I can barely keep my tears back. Let me finish with a scene I saw that is one of the most heartbreaking scenes I have ever witnessed.

A reporter is going around asking people where they are from and if they have lost their homes. A couple in the background, not wanting to face the reporter, is surrounded by a group. The husband is angrily talking to the group of people away from the microphone, and has a little sack on his shoulder, hunched over his back.

Noticing his fury, the reporter is trying to get to him, trying to find out what is going on, why he is so upset. The man is really trying not to talk to her and avoids looking at her. Finally the reporter gets the microphone in the man's face and asks him what is wrong.

He pulls down the little sack and opens it and in it there is a beautiful little girl—dead. He says to the reporter, "I'll tell you what is wrong. I went to every hospital and nobody helped me. The doctor told me that there was nothing he could do—he didn't have medicine or anything."

The man says, "If I were rich my little girl wouldn't have died! I lost my home and now I've lost the only child I had."

He says he later took the dead body to the morgue, and they had so many corpses they told him they couldn't do anything for him and couldn't be responsible for the body. (The whole time the camera is focusing on the dead baby.) The man looks at the reporter and asks her, "So what can I do? Toss her body into the river? I have no money or place to bury her!"

He and his wife begin sobbing. Immediately all these poor people surrounding them, who had also lost everything begin putting money in his pocket, giving this man all they had left.

I hope your heart is as broken as mine is right now. I hope the Lord guides you to pray and aid all these people who have lost everything.

This has all the characteristics of a personal master story. At the same time, it takes place within the larger master story of his faith in God. You can sense that this personal story both creates tension with his larger story (why such suffering for those who already suffer so much?), and at the same time, the larger story of faith tells him how to respond to what is happening in this present-tense story (prayer, volunteering, compassion).

Still in the Midst of Our Own Story

Our master stories are never *over*. We continue to live within them until the day we die—and after. They are part of our own ongoing story in which we are still characters—doing, reflecting, analyzing, criticizing, modifying (which to say, *living*)—up to our last breath. We do not fully know the meaning of our own story as we live it. The goal of legacy work is to provide a nurturing story, perhaps even a master story, for someone else's life. By such, we also give meaning to our own.

6

How to Tell a Good Story

Writing is a second chance at life. Although we can never go back in time to change the past, we can re-experience, interpret, and make peace with our past lives. . . . Writing sometimes seems to me to be the only way to give shape to life, to complete the process which is merely begun by living.

J. McDonald

Everyone, I have claimed, has the ability to tell a story, and particularly a story from their own life. You do not have to be taught how to tell a story, or need "five secrets to good storytelling" articles, or advice from people like me. Telling stories is as natural as breathing, and you have been doing it since before you could talk (pointing and crying and making faces being among our first storytelling strategies).

At the same time, it can be helpful to identify some of the characteristics of a well-told story—both as we think about what to include and when we revise what we have already written. The goal is *not* to write according to a formula but to point in some useful directions.

115

What follows is intended to help you accentuate what you already do naturally and to increase your confidence when you are on the right track. If you find that this is *not* helping, then skip this chapter and tell your stories in your own words and in your own ways.

Moving from Telling to Writing

Consciousness is both a necessity and a curse when writing. Pens, pencils, and keyboards are sometimes paralyzing. Blank computer screens or pieces of paper can be mind numbing. Many are the high-spirited, articulate oral storytellers who become timid and self-conscious when trying to write down what they so easily speak. We have this deep-seated misconception that anyone can talk but only writers can write—as though putting our story on paper puts us in competition with Tolstoy.

Let it go. You're not competing with Tolstoy. You're competing with *oblivion*, which is what you'll have if you don't pass on your stories. Any story, whether beautifully or primitively written, is a strike against being forgotten.

And that leads to the first bit of advice. *If you are having difficulty knowing how to write a story, then write it the same way you would tell it.* Maybe even tell it out loud—to someone else or into a recording device—then transcribe it. This will not result in the very best written version of the story—speaking and writing being different media with different strategies—but it will get something down you can work with.

Writing Before You Write

A second initial bit of advice: *write before you write.* That is, engage in what is sometimes called prewriting or freewriting—old-fashioned brainstorming. If your story focuses on a character, for instance, jot down (as in the exercise in chapter 4) what comes into your mind when you think of that person: physical attributes, sound of voice, personality, favorite expressions, character traits, memorable interactions, influences on you, and so on.

You can also freewrite about setting, the main action of the story, reflections on its meaning, bits of dialogue, what you feel about it, and other aspects of a story. At this initial point, don't worry about where the story starts or how it ends or even whether it is significant. The writing is "free" here because there are no limitations, no judgments, no risks. You are simply stockpiling raw material out of which the story will later be made. Some of it you will use and some you won't, but having it is comforting when you eventually begin to write the story.

When you think you have enough raw material, cluster it into categories such as those suggested above—material related to characters, setting, plot, meaning, and other aspects of the story. Then begin to tell the story, starting anywhere you like. Don't try to get in all the raw material, just the things that insist on being in this particular story. The rest can wait for another story at another time.

A Good Story—on Many Fronts

Because I want all the guidelines covered in this chapter to be of practical help, we will start with a story that will be used to illustrate what follows. Titled "Lists," this story was written by Carmen Williams, a woman in her fifties. It has some of the attributes of a master story, as discussed in the last chapter, but is offered here simply as a well-told story from which we can learn about good writing.

> Lists. I like making them but the greater enjoyment comes in checking off each line, each task completed.
>
> Schedules. The routine of a schedule gives order to my life and a feeling of control. My lists and schedules comfortably hold each other's hands, and I must confess the annoyance of unannounced interruptions that come to either.
>
> October 8, 1999 is a date that marks the beginning of many unsolicited interruptions, each one marching into my life with bold arrogance.
>
> "You have a large mass . . ." says the technician, and the rest of his words trail off into space.
>
> Until then, cancer was just a word—a disease that others were diagnosed with. Suddenly my life stands frozen and the lists

and schedules retreat with the stark realization that "control" was only an illusion.

A month and a half passes. Surgery, recovery, and my first chemo treatment are behind me. Soon my hair will be gone. Why am I not coping with something I expected? Perhaps it's because all that's been connected with cancer, so far, has been invisible. Baldness is a visible sign of this disease. My medical team consoles me with logic; if the chemotherapy is killing the "good" fast-growing cells (as in hair cells), it is killing the "bad" fast-growing cancer as well.

The morning begins as a "bad hair day" as I prepare for another visit to the doctor. I was told that I'd lose my hair, but the knowledge doesn't diminish the feelings of horror as I scoop handfuls of hair from the bottom of the bathtub. So much is falling out and yet stubborn strands remain intact.

By evening it's quite thin and my scalp is a patchwork of tufts and spaces. I feel as though I'm losing my mind along with my hair. On the back stoop of our home I frantically rake my fingers through what's left in a desperate attempt to be rid of all of it! Hair falls in clumps around my feet. Returning to the house with my mind feeling somewhat detached from the body, my hands continue to work independently, flitting to my head like little birds returning to their homes in the tree tops. It's time to make a phone call to my friend.

I call her "Nurse Didi." Her name is Diane and she is not a nurse—but she is a servant of the highest calling. We have been friends for thirty-five years and she has always been a part of my faith story, woven into the threads that create the tapestry of my life.

"Would you like me to come over and cut what's left?" she softly asks.

"I don't know . . ." is my response.

"You might feel better about the loss if you involve yourself in it," she says. "I'll come first thing in the morning, but it's entirely up to you."

She comes with her tools—a sharp scissors, an electric shaver and a heart full of love. I sit on the metal stool that stood for years in my mother's kitchen like a dutiful nanny, holding

118

the behinds of little children who ate donuts at her table. But this is no treat. It's pure anguish and I am coping by chanting over and over, "I-can-do-all-things-through-Christ-who-strengthens-me," like it's a mantra instead of a Bible verse to settle my heart. My friend doesn't waste words, but snips away at the thin patches of hair still left on my head and then carefully and tenderly shaves the rest.

My chanting drifts to memories of our son, Ross, getting his hair cut as a little boy, sometimes while sitting on his father's lap. And that's where I'm really seated this morning—on my heavenly Father's lap, feeling quite at peace, finally, as Didi lovingly does what needs to be done.

What Makes a Good Story Good

So you've got a story in mind to write, you have slain the inner critic. Now how can you tell the story in a way that is most likely to draw others in? Here is some guidance, but take it all with a large grain of salt. Use the helpful parts and ignore the rest.

Character and Action

We are most interested in stories about other human beings. Center your story on a character—likely a single character, two at the most. There can be more than two characters, of course, but dividing the primary focus beyond two usually dilutes the story's energy. In the story above, there is one primary character and a significant supporting character. In a longer story you could have a second central figure and more supporting characters, but readers will have trouble keeping track of characters who do not impinge on the action, so keep the supporting cast to a minimum. Even if lots of people were in the room when your story happened, we don't need to meet them all.

Describe that central character to us in some detail. You may have a clear mental image of the person in your head, but the reader may have only a blank space until you describe what that character looks, sounds, and acts like. You don't have to do all the description at once.

119

It can be effective to add descriptive details throughout a story, building a character bit by bit.

Descriptions do not have to be exhaustive, and it can slow a story down too much if the reader feels you are halting the flow of the story in order to give fat paragraphs of character description. In the story above the only *physical* character description is the hair falling out, which is skillfully described. But there is much more *psychological* description of her state of mind, which is, in fact, the core of the story.

The most interesting characters do something. Stories require an *action*. An abstract description of Aunt Bee as a certain kind of lady may have some value, but *show* us Aunt Bee in action, actually doing and saying things, and you have the makings of an engaging story. If her actions are the central action of the story, so much the better. In the story above, the main overarching action is the speaker dealing inwardly with the fact of her cancer and the changes it brings into her life. It culminates in a physical action, cutting off her hair, which is both mundane and powerfully symbolic.

You may or may not be a character yourself in some of the stories you need to tell. The story above is a first-person account (told, interestingly, in the present tense, giving it more immediacy) of a deeply personal time in the teller's life. But she also has stories to tell in which she is not the main character, or perhaps even a character at all. My father told me stories about watching Jackie Robinson play basketball (yes, basketball) in which my father was only a spectator. It wasn't a story about my father, though the way he told it did, of course, reveal something about him.

Sometimes our role is simply to pass on an important family story from a previous generation. We were not there, we did not even know the people who were there, but it is an important story, and our job is to keep it moving down the generations.

Of course you often will turn out to be the main character in one of your stories. When that happens, it may help to think of yourself as just another character rather than being hyperconscious of writing about yourself. A little detachment can help both the effectiveness and truthfulness of the story. Remember, you don't have to show this story to anyone if you do not choose to. Look at yourself with the same compassionate honesty that you look at any other character in your stories.

EXERCISE ONE

Choose a story from one of your lists.

Identify the central character or characters in your story, and then the supporting characters.

Freewrite about them all, jotting down key characteristics of all kinds: physical, psychological, emotional, and otherwise. Identify the characteristics that might be most relevant to the particular story you have in mind.

Freewrite about the different ways you can offer insights into the character in your story—through description, dialogue, action, reflections, and the like.

EXERCISE TWO

Identify the central action of the story from exercise 1. What is the main *event* of the story? Is it an external or internal action—or both?

Summarize what that main action is in a few sentences.

Identify which characters are most important to the action and which are supporting characters.

Scenes

Organize your story around scenes. Houses are built with two-by-fours, and stories are built with scenes. A scene is simply something happening to characters in a setting. A long story is composed of a series of scenes. (Each scene is a story within the story—like acts in a play.) A brief story may be a single scene with a single character and a single action.

A scene is usually dramatic—not necessarily in the sense of tense action but in the sense of people interacting, either with other people or with the setting or with their inner selves. The action in a scene may seem like no action at all. It can be anything from rescuing a damsel in distress (or escaping a sinking ship at Pearl Harbor), to a quiet conversation between two people, to a person looking out the window and thinking.

The power of scenes is that they lure us into becoming a member of the scene ourselves. Abstractions give us information; scenes put us in the middle of an action. We are called to witness, to see something unfolding, to feel, and to make judgments—in short, to be part of the story, even if it happened long ago. Even when a scene is written in the past tense, it plays out in the head of the reader in the present tense, as though the reader is witnessing the action as it is happening.

The opposite of scene is summary, and summary has its uses. Summary is abstract discussion as opposed to dramatic action. The following could be a slice from my own childhood: "My father liked to spend money we didn't have, and that was a problem in my parents' marriage the whole time I was growing up." That is a true statement, and I could see myself writing it in a story about my childhood. But compare it with the following: "My father came up the driveway carrying a big, new television. My mother met him at the door and said, 'If that thing comes in the front door, then I'm leaving out the back door.'"

The first is a summary statement, and the latter is a two-sentence scene. They both might be appropriate at a given point in a life story, but the scene is the one that is going to more fully engage a reader. The combination of setting, characters, and action puts us on the porch between my father in the driveway and my mother at the door, and we can't help but want to know what happens next.

Stories often need summary as well as scene. Summary allows you to cover larger stretches of time, give overviews, provide opportunities for reflection, and get quickly from one scene to another. But a story that is mostly summary is likely to be mostly boring—or at least less engaging than it should be. When we tell stories we naturally gravitate toward setting a scene and then letting the scene play out.

The story about the haircut above uses both scene and summary. It starts with a generalization about the writer's love of lists and schedules, but then moves quickly to a specific date: October 8, 1999. It gives us just a glimpse of a scene from that day, reduced to only the medical technician's few words about "a large mass." But that is enough, because in fact those words block out everything else, including further details about the scene. She has struck to the core of the scene and the action, and we are hooked.

The writer then returns to generalized reflections on the disruption the discovery of cancer has made on her list-loving life. This is summary and reflection that grows out of the scene she has briefly sketched. One leads to another, and then the reflection leads back to another brief scene, signaled by the summary transition: "A month and a half passes." We don't need to know anything about those six weeks; stories always leave out much more than they put in. We need to get to the next scene, and the summary sentence gets us there.

The next scene is three paragraphs long and includes helpful bits of dialogue so we hear the characters' voices. It stretches over a full day, starting with scooping hair from the bathtub in the morning to making a phone call to her friend at night. It has action, dialogue, setting, and it reveals the delicate psychological state of the main character.

That scene is followed by another, the central scene of the story. It mixes effective, understated description—of both external and internal action—with reflection. And it comes to a sense of ending—a kind of closure that does not pretend to "answer" the problems raised by suffering but that offers us a better understanding of such experiences than we had (and perhaps than the writer had) before she began telling her story.

EXERCISE THREE

Think about a story you wish to write in terms of scene.

How many scenes do you expect there to be? Where do you surmise each will take place? Who will be in the scene? What will be the main thing that happens in the scene?

If there is more than one scene, what order might they come in and how might you get from one to the other?

At what point might you want to add space for reflection and chewing on what you are describing?

Note: It can be helpful to think about scenes before you write a story, but understand that you may well not be able to answer all these questions in advance. Many things only come to us as we actually write the story.

Dialogue

Whenever we hear an individual voice, in public or in private, we tend to pay attention to it. The same is true in story. We are drawn to the sound of the speaking voice, and so effective stories usually let us hear people talking.

We hear written dialogue in our head just as surely as we hear spoken words with our ears. Hearing people speak is one of the ways in which a story convinces us that it is true. It helps us "be there," feel like we are witnessing an event, not just receiving a report.

Talking is a form of action. We *do* things to each other with our words. Spoken words can be weapons and they can be salve for wounds. Even not talking is a form of action, especially in a situation where people normally talk.

Dialogue is also an important way in which to reveal character. We define much of our relationship to the world and to others by what we say—and by how we say it. If you want us to feel we know a character, let us hear that person speak.

Which raises the question, what if we don't remember or know exactly what was said? This is an ethical as well as a craft question. In private life, as in history, we rarely have a recording of spoken words. Is it okay to put words in people's mouths if you're not sure that's exactly what was said? My answer, and that of most memoirists, is yes, within certain boundaries.

You can present a person's words as dialogue if any of the following conditions are met. The words contain the essence of a conversation you yourself witnessed. Or if the words are indicated as the reported memory of someone else—if that is, in fact, how you received the information. (If you have some doubts about the accuracy of the report, say so.) Or if they are in keeping with what you believe to be true about the character you are presenting and how that person typically speaks.

It is not permissible in life writing (though it is in fiction writing) to *invent* long speeches for characters, or to have them say out loud what you or someone else believes they were thinking. As a writer of memoir, you are free to speculate and evaluate, but you are not free to create "evidence" for your speculations out of nothing. Your aunt may well have wanted to tell your uncle that he was a lecherous old drunk, but if she didn't say it out loud, don't put the words in her mouth. (Instead describe the look on her face, which might be more effective anyway.)

Sometimes you can report on a character's favorite expressions without attaching them to a specific event or setting: "Grandpa liked to say, 'You can tell a lot about a man by the way he keeps his tackle box.'"

A sort of middle ground between straight reporting and ethically doubtful fabrication is to come clean in your writing that you are giving it your best shot, but not guaranteeing court-reporting accuracy. Phrases like, "As best I can remember . . ." or "She said something like . . ." or "The family story is that he replied . . ." go a long way toward winning you the license you need to tell the story the best you can. Readers want a good story that is *essentially* true (see "Telling the Truth" below); they will cut you lots of slack on how you get there.

Although dialogue enlivens storytelling, you should use it only in snatches unless you are good at it. Direct speech is usually short, often with incomplete sentences, because we don't normally let people make long speeches in our presence, especially if we are irritated. Sometimes you can spice a summary report of a conversation with just a few words of actual speech, and the reader is satisfied that they have heard someone's voice.

That is what the writer does in the "Lists" story above. She gives us just the beginning of one sentence from the technician, "You have a large mass . . . ," and we easily imagine the setting and the rest of the conversation. We don't need more, but we did need that small bit.

Then there is a longer exchange between the speaker and her friend Didi. Only three sentences long, the exchange nevertheless humanizes this supporting character, makes us feel we are also on the phone when the conversation takes place, and conveys the ambivalence within the narrator. It is much more effective than merely saying, "I called my friend and she came over."

EXERCISE FOUR

Take a story you have already written and look for places where dialogue could be added to increase interest—for example, where you have summarized an exchange between characters instead of giving the actual words.

Turn the summary into dialogue.

Setting

All stories happen somewhere—and many times that place is itself an important part of the story. *Somewhere* is both a place and a time. All of the following can contribute to the setting of a story, and thereby to its impact and significance: the specific space (for example, a room or garden or boat), the wider geographical place (a desert, Times Square, the South, at sea), the historical period (the Depression, World War II or Desert Storm, the collapse of Communism), the time of day (the same event feels different at night than it would in the daylight), the season (think of the common associations with spring), the cultural context (a religious subculture, the 1960s), and so on. All of these externals are part of the setting and help shape a story and the characters within it.

A setting is not just background scenery. It provides the context in which things happen to people and is itself part of what is happening. That's why it's worth spending time conveying the setting. If you are telling a story about war, give your reader a feeling for what war looks and smells and sounds like. If it is a story about church, what kind of building did you go to church in, and what might the kind of building tell us about the people worshiping in it? What kind of music? How did people dress?

Settings can themselves become characters in a story. If you are writing about shoveling during a blizzard, the blizzard is a character and

126

deserves some attention (see Vivien Steinbach's story in the appendix). Same with an office cubicle—especially if you love or hate it.

Settings can also reveal character. We are shaped in part by our surroundings, but we also impose ourselves upon those surroundings. Some grandmothers can be better understood through a description of their kitchens, as others might be revealed through a description of their bedrooms, offices, workshops, gardens, cars, or icehouses.

So when you try to tell a story, ask if settings have a role to play. Remember that all life stories happen in the past, and many of them happen in a past not shared by the reader (or even the storyteller). Don't assume readers know and understand the significance of the setting any more than you would assume they know the character. A good story gives us both and shows the linkage between the two.

There are two settings in the "Lists" story: a medical setting and a home setting. The medical setting, again, is treated very briefly but effectively. Because she gives us a few of the words spoken there, we are in the room when the medical technician gives her the bad news. But home is the more important setting, because it is the place she spends most of her time. And it is the place in which she has to come to terms with her illness. We get brief references to the details of this place: a bath tub, a back stoop, the phone. But the most important part of the setting is that metal stool, the one that once was in her mother's kitchen, and on which she now sits while her head is shaved by her friend. It is not an impressive bit of "setting" in itself, but as she sits on it and thinks of her son sitting on his father's lap years before, it becomes the vehicle by which she transmits the central insight of the story. Without the detail of the stool, the story is diminished.

EXERCISE FIVE

Make a list of places or settings that have been significant for you. Include both large-scale settings (cities, mountains, lakes, deserts, buildings, ruins) and intimate settings (rooms, a garden, a favorite chair).

Freewrite about that setting. List details that come to mind.

Use the freewriting material to write a description of it.

Reflect in writing on the significance of the setting to you.

EXERCISE SIX

Describe in detail a place associated with a person in a way that reveals the personality or values or actions of that person.

Try doing so without having that person present in the setting.

Then do it again, adding that person going about typical activities in that setting.

Consider, as examples, the following settings: kitchen, workshop, garden, fishing boat, bedroom, desk, car, church pew.

Description and Revealing Details

If scenes are the two-by-fours of stories, then description is the nails. Most of what takes place in a story is described to us, and describing well is a key to good storytelling.

Description is primarily an account of something in terms of the senses: what something looked, sounded, felt, tasted, or smelled like, or how it moved. The brain uses the senses to make contact with and understand the external world, so when a story appeals to our senses, it is giving the brain what it is familiar with. Description creates the sense that what is being described is *real*—even if it is fairies or talking bears.

If a story doesn't have enough description, then it remains abstract and distant. (If it has too much, the details overgrow the story like a tangle of vines.) Storytellers need to remember that the supporting details in their own heads are usually not in the heads of their audience. A story may seem rich in detail to you because you are visualizing and hearing it as you tell it. But that richness is shared by the reader only if you take the time to describe that world in detail. Look back at that description of getting up and catching the bus in the morning in chapter 4. It is effective because it gives us the descriptive details—sight, sound, smell, taste, and touch—of a farmhouse on a typical school-day morning in winter.

Any detail that helps create the world of the story can be helpful, but there is one kind of detail that is particularly valuable—the revelatory detail. A revelatory or significant or luminous detail is one that provides immediate *insight* into a person or situation or event. It may seem small, even insignificant, but for the perceptive reader it reveals something.

In the city of Vienna, for example, there was, when I visited many years ago, a government-provided phone number you could call that did nothing but play the musical note A. So what? That's a detail one could mention in talking about Vienna, but why do so? What does the detail reveal? It reveals a lot. It tells us that this is a city and a culture that values music, a key part of its own spiritual legacy. This culture supports music in many ways, one small example of which is providing a service so that any musician in the city—and there are many of them—could call this number and tune his or her instrument. This small revelatory detail tells us something significant about a key value for an entire society.

Human beings are always giving off revealing signals about what they are thinking or feeling or valuing. As was suggested above when talking about setting, the details of a person's office or bedroom or garage will silently reveal much about that person's values, personality, and character. So do a person's verbal habits or facial expressions or manner of buttering toast. The more of these you include, the stronger your story will be.

But don't go off the descriptive deep end. Don't pile up paragraphs of description just because you know how to do it. One nineteenth-century French writer opened a novel with a hundred-page description of the front of a house. One such story is enough. Use description only to enhance the effectiveness of the story. Describe the weather if the weather plays a role or helps set the mood, but skip it otherwise. Describe the mole between your math teacher's eyebrows, because that was the thing you were thinking about when you didn't notice that he had called your name.

"Lists" uses description sparingly but well. Look at the two paragraphs about the author's hair falling out. The writer doesn't simply say, "My hair fell out." She describes a particular day when it falls out in bunches, leaving "a patchwork of tufts and spaces." She uses figurative language in describing herself "raking" her head with her fingers. By skillful description the writer makes us feel the desperation we might experience if our own hair was suddenly falling out. These details and others do not simply create a setting; they reveal a state of mind.

Describe in order to help create the world of your story for your reader, but prize above all the luminous details that reveal something.

EXERCISE SEVEN

Look at some of the other exercises you have done that require description (of a character or a setting, for instance).

Find (or create for the first time) details in those descriptions that are especially revealing of something. Identify what insight or revelation they provide.

Then rewrite the description to provide even more revealing details.

Strong Openings

No sentence or paragraph in a story is more important than the first one. It begins the transition for the reader from his or her world into the world of the story. It needs to be strong and engaging so that the transition takes place quickly.

Too often life stories start off weakly. Sometimes they beat around the bush, talking about the *prospect* of telling a story rather than starting the story itself. Other times they fail to make clear the where, when, and who of the story (though total clarity can wait a bit). Often they begin abstractly or apologetically ("I'm a pretty lousy writer, and I can't spell worth beans.")

Start instead with one of the following: a strong description, an interesting assertion, a mysterious hint of what's to come, a character speaking, a humorous observation, a beautiful metaphor or other interesting figure of speech, a powerful setting, or anything else likely to make a sleepy reader sit up and take notice.

Understand also that stories very often do not start at the earliest chronological point. The usual advice is to start close to the most important action, and then fill in earlier material later as needed. In telling the story of your father's life, you could easily begin in his hospital room at the end of his life, and then move backward to tell us what kind of person he was.

Compare the following two openings:

> We took a lot of vacations when I was a kid. Vacations were fun. They gave us a chance to get away from home. I don't really remember much about most of them, but some of them I remember better.

No obvious errors in that opening, but also very little of interest. It announces a topic—vacations—but that's about all. It certainly doesn't distract the reader from wondering what's on television. Compare it with the following:

> "The tent is leaking! My sleeping bag is soaked and I'm freezing! I wanna go home!" I was seven years old, we were camping in the Adirondack Mountains, and I was an unhappy camper. My parents just looked at me and laughed, and invited me to climb into one of their sleeping bags. They loved our family vacations, disasters and all, and so, eventually, did I.

The second example starts in the middle of an action. It puts us in a scene with something going on. It gives us details, dialogue, and reflection. It has characters and relationships and human nature. It hints of disaster stories to come and has a touch of humor. The reader will definitely go on to the next paragraph.

Consider the following strong opening from a story by Ed Ericson Jr. about his father:

> When he was sixteen, he threw his father down the eight steps from the front porch to the sidewalk. That same year, when his father awakened him on a Sunday morning to get ready for church, he stood up and said, "Dad, I'm not going today, and I'm not going ever again. I'm bigger than you now, and you can't make me." And he kept his word for the next sixteen years, not going to church even to get married.

The reader is hooked, and the ground is laid for the first sentence of the next paragraph.

> Fast-forward a quarter century and see the now middle-aged white man standing in the midst of a bunch of black kids at a Sunday school he superintends on the worst Skid Row in Chicago.

As important as the opening is, you do not need to think much about it until you are ready to revise your story. It's not until then that you even need to decide where your story starts. As we've seen, the first draft of a story can start anywhere. Later you can decide if that is, in fact, the best place to start, or whether something else should come before it.

But once you have decided where you are going to open, make it as strong and engaging as you can.

EXERCISE EIGHT

Choose a story of which you've already written at least a draft. (Or look at one of the stories in this book.)

Evaluate the opening sentence and paragraph. How could it be better?

Write a new one, making it as engaging as possible. Consciously identify the strategies you are using to make it so.

Telling the Truth

We come up with all sorts of words to describe and evaluate a successful story: entertaining, enjoyable, funny, pleasant. If a story strikes us at a deeper level we use additional words: powerful, moving, meaningful, engaging, haunting, compelling, significant—even life-changing. These are words that suggest that an effective story does exactly that—it affects (and effects) us, changes us, leaves us in a different place, maybe leaves us even a slightly different person than we were before *experiencing* (not just hearing or reading) the story.

All of these words, especially those in the second list, speak to what I believe is at the heart of all important stories—truth. This is not a fashionable claim these days, and I want to make clear what I mean by it. I also want to make clear that I do *not* think a writer, amateur or professional, should *think* about any of this when writing. Thinking too much about truth, not to mention Truth, can clog the creative pores and turn good stories into pale sermons. Truth is real, but it is also shy and comes at no one's whistle.

Thinking about truth can help us, however, when we look back over what we have written. It can help us recognize the good parts and why they are good, and help us recognize the weak parts and give us a rationale for improving them or quietly cutting them out.

All of what follows is abstract, but each of these kinds of truth can be found in the stories used in this book. There are, I believe, at least six levels of truth in stories, and sometimes one story will have them all.

Factual Truth

Factual truth is simply external accuracy—the who, what, when, and where of journalistic reporting. It requires being as reliable as possible about the data that surrounds and infuses a story. Sometimes you can get a couple of these journalistic facts into a story but not all. I remember, for instance, getting out of the back seat of a car as a child, in the driveway of my house in the lemon orchard, and my large grandmother getting out of the front seat and turning fiercely to me and saying, "Don't you story to me," with an emphasis on "me." I can't say for sure, however, when it happened. I was likely four or five years old (since we moved away when I was still five), but the important thing is not exactly when (a factual truth) but that this was my first exposure to the notion that stories could be considered lies.

In storytelling, factual truth is the least important kind of truth, but it has its place. Being right about the facts protects against deeper truths being passed over by a reader because you've been careless with the basics. If you mistakenly add Uncle John to the scene of a story about an event that shaped you, you risk a dismissive wave of the hand, "Uncle John wasn't even there. He was still in Germany then.

You don't know what you're talking about." You may know very well what you're talking about, but getting that secondary fact wrong undercuts your credibility.

Sometimes a little research helps. What was that number one song in 1962? When, exactly, was World War II over? What was the name of the high school where your grandmother taught music for thirty years? These are facts that you can find out. And if finding out helps your story, then look it up. If it doesn't, then don't bother. But don't pretend you know if you don't. Facts matter—a bit.

Experiential Truth

Experiential truth is, for lack of a more precise description, the "feel of life" in a piece of writing. When we read something, in any genre, that seems to embody a part of what we have ourselves experienced in life, we are compelled to give it our assent, at least for the moment. We say, "Yes, that is how life is," or, "I have felt that myself," or, "That's what cat owners are like."

Experiential truth is a form of accuracy, but it is not primarily factual accuracy. Some stories are filled with realistic detail—every fact in place—yet devoid of the feel of actual human experience. Experiential truth is holistic—as is all story truth. It involves the mind and emotions and body.

It also is not propositional. It doesn't convince you of a specific assertion about life; it simply gives you the feel that it partakes of life itself and that it is offering you the opportunity to partake as well. If you tell the story of your mother greeting your dad when he came home from a war, it will help to get the year and month right, a tip of the hat to factual truth. But if you want it to feel like life, include her trying out four different colors of lipstick before he walks in the door.

Philosophical Truth

Philosophical truth is general insight into the nature of the human condition and human experience. It helps us sort out what is actual, what is illusion, and what is false. Philosophical truth is expressed in claims. It says, "This is real," and, "This is more important than that," and, "This is something you need to know to live well."

Philosophical truth is one source of shoulds and oughts, and good stories are full of both. Spiritual legacy stories, in particular, are concerned with providing us resources that help us live well. We often fantasize, especially when young, about living in a situation in which "no one can tell me what to do." Spiritual legacy stories believe otherwise. They try, as best they can, to provide guidance about what, in fact, we should do. Guidance, not commands.

The traditional goal of philosophical truth is to help us live wisely. When we learn something from a story, directly or indirectly, that helps us make wise choices in life or gives us peace about who we are, we are the better for it. When I tell my children the story of my asking a disabled girl to dance in sixth grade, I am not simply offering a bit of sentimental entertainment; I am offering them my understanding of how best to live.

Emotional Truth

Emotional truth is an accurate and nuanced presentation of how the teller or the people within a story feel about the events of the story. It is crucial in all nontechnical writing, nowhere more so than in telling stories from life. When we say that a story "rings true," we are often speaking of the truth of the emotions—it *feels* right.

Conveying the truth of the emotions requires both emotional intelligence and emotional honesty. Emotional intelligence is being perceptive about the emotional resonance inherent in relationships—a keen sense of how people are *affected* by things and how they display that in a myriad of ways. Sometimes we speak our feelings; more often we convey them by a look on the face, a turning of the head, or by what we do with our hands. Someone with emotional intelligence reads all these signs and responds appropriately. A good storyteller puts these clues in the story.

Emotional honesty is conveying how you actually feel or felt about something rather than how you believe you were supposed to feel, or you wish you had felt (more heroic or saintly, for instance). This can be difficult for at least three categories of people: nice people, religious people, and men. Nice people don't want to hurt anyone's feelings. Religious people have often been conditioned to accept many things without complaint (or even reflection) and to put a positive spin on all pain and suffering. And men, it goes without saying, have typically been socialized to associate emotion with weakness.

Emotional truth does not require emotionalism or sentimentality, which are exaggerations of emotion beyond what a situation calls for (admittedly a subjective judgment). Emotional truth simply recognizes that what we feel about a situation is as important as what we think about it and that thinking and feeling are usually mixed inextricably together. If you do not include the truth of the emotions—either those of the time or how you feel about it now—then you are shortchanging both the factual and the experiential aspects of truth, because both of these include the emotions.

Emotional honesty, I want quickly to add, is not, however, an excuse for hostility. Too often we use the phrase "I'm just being honest" as a phony ethical cover for dumping venomously on someone else—living or dead. Honesty should be married to humility and grace. You can baldly state how you felt or how you feel—even in harsh terms—but you should follow it with a show of understanding that others are not here to tell their side of the story. Spiritual legacy work is a place for understanding, grace, and forgiveness, not for revenge.

Annie Dillard, who has mined her life as powerfully as anyone, says, "I don't believe in a writer's kicking around people who don't have access to a printing press. They can't defend themselves." That's a good principle for all spiritual legacy work. This is not the place to get even. Your reader will think less of you for trying.

Spiritual Truth

By spiritual truth I mean anything that connects us with and gives us insight into genuine transcendence. Each of these key terms—*spiritual, truth, transcendence*—is difficult to define and impossible to do complete justice to. It is telling that this highest and most desirable kind of truth is the one least amenable to our categorization and control.

136

I do not limit spiritual truth to religious truth—religion being too small a category for transcendence. Spiritual truth includes realities that are bigger than any of us individually or all of us collectively. It connects us with ultimate things, with those things that are at the center of reality and beyond the edge of the material. If you don't believe there is anything beyond the material, then I believe the highest truth you can hope for is psychological, not spiritual, truth.

For me, all things spiritual—in a healthy sense—are rooted in God. But a story can partake of the spiritual without ever mentioning God. God's Spirit suffuses creation and human lives (while also remaining distinct from them), so whenever we are getting to the deepest—and highest—levels of either, we are in the realm of the spiritual. I can tell many worthwhile stories about my life and the people in it, but I cannot tell the most important ones without dealing with the spiritual.

Reaching for spiritual truth in a story, however, is not a license for lecturing, preaching, or pious clichés. Nothing kills a story faster than the sense that the story is just a cover for a speech. Reflection is often desirable in a spiritual legacy story, but it best takes the form of the teller probing the experience for *personal* significance. That is different from using the story as mere illustration for a finger-wagging sermonette.

The principle here, as in so much of storytelling, is *trust the story.* Let the story do the work. It embodies in itself all the truths you hope to pass on. Tell the story the best you can, reflect on it if useful, then get out of the way.

The Truth of Craft

I believe spiritual truth is the highest kind, but I want to at least mention one other—truth to language and to the craft of writing. I hesitate to include this because thinking too much about which words you are using may create a paralyzing self-consciousness that is the enemy of good storytelling. My advice to most people doing spiritual legacy work is to forget about words and just tell the story. But to some, however, I would add, until you revise. (See chapter 9 for more on revision.)

Caring about language and the shape of stories will get you thinking about issues like economy (making every word carry weight and getting rid of those that don't), strong verbs, figurative language, strong openings and closings, rhythm, structure, luminous details, voice, point of view, and many other things. There are lots of books about such matters, so I will not explore them here. But I will say that having respect for language is also a legacy issue—it is passed on to us from others who have valued its skillful and honorable use, and it is worthwhile to try to do the same.

I considered including one more kind of truth—interpretative truth. This is the truth that comes from trying to make sense of the raw data of the senses that flow over and through us. Human beings are interpretive, meaning-making creatures. We are constantly trying to figure life out, to ascribe significance, to make things fit, to connect one thing to another. All this is at the heart of storytelling.

But in my view, interpretation is inherent in all the categories of truth, not something separable from them. We cannot help but interpret, to offer an understanding, and every good story will do so. Even when we claim that we understand nothing, or that life is meaningless, that is itself an interpretation and a claim about the truth of things. We tell our stories to speak the truth as we see it—in all the ways discussed above—and we offer them to others in hopes that our truths will be helpful.

Look again at the "Lists" story. I believe it has all the forms of truth I have discussed. I assume its factual truth without having any way to confirm it, but with no concerns that it is not accurate at that most basic level. It passes the test of experiential truth because it has the feel of how life actually is—both physically and psychologically—without varnish or pretense. It embodies philosophical truth because it gives insight into the human condition and how we deal with pain. It conveys emotional truth because of its vulnerability and honesty about how circumstances feel. And it reaches the level of spiritual truth by finding within the experience the presence of God and ultimate things.

Finally, the story is true to the demands of the craft. It pays attention to pace and rhythm, it begins and ends strongly, it exploits the possibilities of metaphor and simile ("My lists and schedules comfortably hold each other's hand"; hands "flitting to my head like little birds returning to their homes in the tree tops"). The story uses dialogue and present tense to create immediacy, uses word economically and precisely, and generally shows respect for language and the craft of storytelling.

And it does all that we have talked about, here and elsewhere, in one page. A story does not have to be long to be successful—on many levels. This story shows the emptiness of the commonplace excuse, "I don't have time." No time for one page? Not even when somebody you love needs the story?

7

Dealing with Pain and Painful People

A Story of My Own

Memoir—the long voice telling its tale—can rouse sleeping dogs that others would rather let lie.

Annette Kobak

Storytelling is the ointment of the Healer.

Roy Henry (Native American)

I need to practice what I preach. So here is a story of my own. It deals with pain and painful people. It is, in that sense, a sad story, though it is searching for something more helpful than sadness. The story raises issues about how to deal with painful topics and the ethics of writing about your life, which I'll address afterward. I call the story, "I Tell My Mother Lies."

> I tell my mother lies.
> Sometimes three or four times a day.

I lie mostly about money. That I've sent it or that I'm just about to send it. Or that surely I will send it tomorrow. My mother waits for money like the bums waited for Godot.

One day she called seventeen times. So said the long-distance bill. But I admit I stopped answering after seven or eight. That's not as cruel as it sounds—because each call was new for her. She didn't think, "My son refuses to answer my calls." She thought, "I need money. I'll call Danny." Seventeen times.

That's what most every call is about these days—money. It starts with, "Well what's you doing up there?" "Up there" means Minnesota, where I live. She lived for twenty years in Memphis and "up there" made sense. Now she's further north than I am, but she sticks to the old mental map. Good for her.

"Is that wife of yours still running up and down the steps?" She doesn't risk using my wife's name—Jayne. Names are booby traps these days. Try a name and you may reveal the secret—the secret that everyone knows but you.

But eventually—very quickly actually—she gets to the point. "Listen, honey. I am desperate for some money." And she is desperate. That's the stabbing part. She is desperate. You can hear it in her voice. It's full of anxiety and appeal. And you want to do something about it. Your mother is desperate and you want her not to be. You want her to be okay. You want her to be peaceful—full of peace. Because you know that she has earned it, and because she is your mother.

My mother has had to worry about money most all her life. She married an irresponsible man. A talented man. A charming man. In many ways a generous man. But a man you couldn't trust with money. If he had money he spent it—often on himself. You could send him out for bread and milk and he'd come back six hours later with a new television set. Or three new suits (he wanted to look good even when he got fat), or five books (he read to find the world he needed to live in), or, one time, six of those new-fangled transistor radios ("If one breaks, then we've always got another one").

My father didn't make as much as he spent—at any of his fifteen different jobs. We lived, unbeknownst to three trusting little boys, on the ragged edge of insolvency. We were never officially poor, but we sometimes toured the neighborhood. My mother fended off the creditors with monthly five-dollar payments on ravenous debts.

So she went to work, becoming a schoolteacher when I was ten. She got up at five in the morning to clean the house, woke the rest of us at six-thirty, went off to a day of teaching and then came home to make supper and wash clothes. Teaching brought in the dependable income, but it couldn't quite keep her ahead of my father.

So the last thing I want my mom to worry about is money. She's got almost enough herself and I've got more to back that up, so money, for the first time in her life, shouldn't be an issue. It's an issue.

"I've got a list of nineteen things I've got to get. And I haven't got a penny to my name."

It's always nineteen things. Never seventeen, never twenty. Sometimes I ask her what's on the list. It's not a fair question. If she actually has a list, and she probably does, she isn't sure where it is, and asking her to remember what's on it is like asking Mrs. Lindbergh about her baby. (I'm sure hairspray is on it—she has seven cans of it in her closet.)

"What good does it do me to have $38,000 in the bank if I can't spend any of it?"

I take it as a rhetorical question. I don't know where she got the number 38,000. I guess it will do as well as any. It's as good as nineteen, twice as good in fact.

And then the question I dread from the moment I hear the phone ring. "Will you send me some of my money, son?" (She doesn't risk my name anymore either.) "I've just got to get some clothes for summer"—or whatever season, about which she is often wrong. "Will you send me some money?"

That's when I lie. It's the only thing I've knowingly lied about to anyone and it's painful. I try to lie quickly, so we can move on to something else.

"Yes, I'll send some money. No problem, Mom."

But she wants details.

"When are you going to send it?"

"Today, Mom. Tomorrow at the latest."

"How much are you going to send? Can you send fifty dollars?"

Mom, I want to say, I'd send fifty thousand dollars. I'd send you the world. If I thought it would do you any good. Even if I thought it would do you good for an hour. But it won't. We've tried. And it won't do you any good at all.

I used to send money, of course. She always wants cash. Checks are part of a universe she doesn't live in anymore. I sent cash gladly, happy there was some little thing I could do for my mom. I sent it until she no could no longer ever remember getting any. Until she claimed she hadn't gotten anything from me in months.

I've also tried delivering it to her. She's now five hours away by car, closer than when she lived in Memphis. I've memorized the route: north on 94 to 27, then west to 9 and north again to 55, which changes to 11 once it crosses into North Dakota, then all the way to Ellendale on 11, many miles but only a few bends in the road later. Lately I tend to drive there and back in the same day. My brother's place is full and the local motel makes the Bates look like Shangri La.

So when I visit I always bring some twenties. Sometimes I mix in fives and tens to make it look like more, but she's still sharp enough to spot that trick. It's just another way of lying.

She always claims, a claim as predictable as the list of nineteen things, that the money will be safe. "I've got a great place to hide it," she says. "Nobody knows where it is." Nobody—including her. The staff says they find bills everywhere, including inter-leaved within a stack of napkins.

When Mom first got to Evergreen (the name of the facility, itself a kind of lie), she claimed people were stealing from her. She'd whisper into the phone, "The black maids, here . . . they steal." It was disconcerting to hear a long-buried prejudice resurface in a woman who opened her arms and house to everyone over the years. She was raised in Kentucky in the 1920s and '30s, and had absorbed a kind of working class view of race that thought itself perfectly fair. I remember her telling me her own mother's response when my mom asked why their black cook was eating in the dining room while the rest of the family was around the kitchen table: "Why, Nita, we always have our company eat in the dining room."

My mother knew better even as a kid, but now that knowledge, like so much else, has been erased. I try to reason with her, without resorting to pointing out that no black people work at the place, and that none likely even live in her tiny North Dakota town. But reason and facts here, as with many things in her world now, are an enemy to be defeated. She gets defensive, like I'm calling her a liar.

"Son, I know what I'm talking about. My roommate has had nineteen pairs of shoes stolen from her closet." There's that number again.

Once she handed the phone to Alma.

"Yup, Mr. Taylor. You listen to your mother. It's true. They're stealing my shoes. Have a good day, now."

"You too, Alma."

I am happy to say that blaming the non-existent black maids has faded away. And her confidence in her hiding place is absolute. So the last time I visited I asked to see it. I had some money for her, I said, and I wanted to see where she hid it.

I actually did believe she had such a hiding place. She hid money from my father for fifty years. It was the only way to save anything at all for the rainy day—and it rained quite often in our family. She was a pack rat saver—sometimes sticking the stray dollar bill in an unmarked envelope, sometimes using the old trick of change in a jar in the closet, letting it pile up over the year to buy Christmas presents and a tree. Sometimes she secreted it away in a savings account that only she knew about.

Unfortunately, my father learned to depend on her secrets.

"Your mom's got some money squirreled away somewhere," he'd say. "She always does."

I think it made him feel even freer to spend whatever was in his back pocket. Ol' Nita has some more somewhere. The last time he discovered a hidden cache was just a few years before he died. It was five thousand dollars or so she had put, bit by bit, into an annuity of some kind. She had been foolish enough to list it in both their names. He discovered it and cashed the policy and came home with one of the first giant projection screen televisions. The workmen could barely get it in the small room. Perhaps that was the day the last ember of my mom's love for my father went cold.

So hiding money is nothing new to my mom. She takes me into the walk-in closet of her room and opens the third drawer down and picks up the handkerchiefs folded neatly in the back, right corner.

"There" she whispers. "That's where I keep it. Nobody knows." I add in my head, "And dad is dead, so we don't have to worry about him."

Actually, I don't know whether this is really where she hides money—nothing's there now—or whether she has just come up with this place on the spur of the moment because I asked. My mother, you see, has gotten subtle of late. Like the serpent was subtle in the Garden. Subtle because she feels she has to be to keep her secret.

She pretends, for instance, to remember places she no longer remembers, to recall events she no longer recalls, to know faces she know longer knows—including mine.

I once took my French brother-in-law with me on a visit to my mom. We took her to lunch, me driving, her in the front passenger seat, and Gerard in the back.

"Where do you live?" she asks Gerard.

"I live in Minneapolis."

"Oh, I have a son who lives there. Do you know him?"

I don't say, "Mom, that's me. Dan. I'm right here beside you." What would be the point? It would first confuse her and then embarrass her and then hurt her. It would let out the secret. So we all participate in another necessary lie. At least I tell myself it's necessary.

Perhaps I should be happy that my mom is still sharp enough to fake it—to be subtle. But she was never subtle before. She was simple and un-ironic and hardworking, whereas my father was complex and reflective and restless. Among the brothers we used to say that Mom was perfectly matched as a sixth-grade teacher, feeling at home among the jokes and life questions of twelve-year-olds.

She still does her best to feel at home, for once again she lives with simple people like herself.

"It's like being back in the college dorm," she says, almost as often as she speaks of her list. "I've got a good roommate and we all spend time together in the lounge. I didn't want to come here, but now that I'm here I see that it's a pretty good life."

In this respect my mother hasn't changed. She spent a lifetime tracing silver linings in black clouds. Complaining was a sin against God and only made bad times worse. If you had a problem, you simply did whatever there was to do about it until the problem dissipated. If there was nothing to do about it, you did something else instead. Cleaned the house. Went to work. Made lunch for your boys.

Her parents were Kentucky hill folk. They put the stoic in stoical. When my grandfather returned to the hills to see his father after many years, the old man simply pronounced my grandfather's name when he walked in the door, "Sam," and kept on rocking, as though his son had just walked out the door that morning. My mom smiled too much to be called stoic, but she wasted little breath on complaints about her life, at least not in front of me.

Sometimes now, however, her defenses droop. She starts, "I'm not complaining now . . ." and then she complains.

"I haven't seen Mark in weeks. And I never see Connie. They've got that ID thing on their phone and they don't answer when they see it's me. So I call them from a different phone so they don't know."

Very subtle.

It's not true, of course. My brother lives in the same little North Dakota town with his family. It's why my mom is there. One or the other of them sees her most days, and they come to take her on outings a couple of times a week, sometimes more. She is always happy to see them—son or grandson or great-grandson or one of the women of the family. She goes gladly on the outings—shopping, birthday parties, the Homecoming promenade at the high school—but her brain begins erasing the tapes even as they are being recorded, and she is sure, within minutes of returning, that no one comes to see her.

147

Even in her complaining, however, she makes allowances.

"Now don't you say a word to them about this. They're very busy. I don't want to bother them. I'm doing fine."

The silver-lining machine is still pumping.

"I just go to bed at night and thank God that all my kids are doing well. And my grandchildren. And they all love Jesus. Do you realize how rare that is?"

I realize, Mom. And if you think we're all doing well, then I'm not going to say otherwise. Thinking so got you through a bad marriage and maybe it will get you through the slow disintegration of your mind.

And my mother, for the first time in her life, will talk about her marriage now, if, as my wife does, you put the questions to her. We're sitting in Ellendale's one remaining restaurant (since the NoDak café closed down). My mom is shocked anew, as always, at the prices on the menu.

"Three dollars for a hamburger! Son, do you see these prices? Well I'm not paying three dollars for a hamburger. I'm not hungry. I'll just have a salad. Do they have salads?"

I don't know at which point in the past the pricing part of her mind is stuck, but it's not at a time when three dollars was acceptable for a restaurant hamburger.

My wife wants to see if mom's memory of the far past is better than of the recent. She asks about places we lived and relatives and what things were like here or there. My mom bobs and weaves through the questions, mostly deflecting them or changing the subject. But when Jayne asks about her marriage, she is more candid than I have ever heard her.

"Your father liked the ladies," she says with a small (ironic?) smile.

It hurts to hear her say it because I can't believe it doesn't hurt her to speak out loud, maybe for the first time ever, what everyone in the family knows. He didn't just "like the ladies"—he liked the ladies sitting in the pews of the churches he pastored—the one recurring job among the fifteen. Maybe, it just now occurs to me, that was one reason we moved so often.

When she says "Your father liked the ladies," I am immediately jerked back to a phone ringing more than thirty-five

148

years ago. I answer it in the hallway of my college dorm and my mom's voice is shaking on the other end.

"Can you come home, Dan."

"What do you mean? When?"

"Now, Dan. Can you come home now? Can you just be here? Can you bring some schoolwork? I won't bother you. I just need you to be here."

"Sure, Mom. What's wrong?"

"I'm just afraid I'm going to kill myself. I'll be fine. I just need you to be here so that I don't do anything."

So of course I went home. I found her sitting in a chair, trembling. She was holding a letter from one of my father's "ladies." It said very ugly things and my mother's silver-lining machine was in shambles.

We didn't talk about it. She didn't want to. Just said she wanted me to be there so she didn't cut her wrists. Assured me she would be better soon. Just needed me in the house. And so I stayed and pretended to study. And thought about my mom. And about my father. And about why couldn't people get along.

We have never talked of that day since.

So when she mentions my father and the ladies I cringe a bit, because I don't want these to be among the last memories bumping around in her head. But then, as if she can read my mind, she says something comforting.

"I didn't have a good marriage, but I've had a good life."

That sounds right to me.

"I made a life for myself. I focused on you boys. And I had my teaching and my friends at school."

She is smiling now, oblivious even to the outrageous price of hamburgers. I don't think this is blowing smoke. She believes it, and I think it is a wise and accurate summation. Life gave her a painful irritation, largely in the form of my father, himself a wounded man, and she encircled that pain with busyness and directed her love to others and, somehow, ended up with what could pass as a pearl.

Directed love is an apt phrase for how my mother related to us and to the world. She wasn't smart enough, to be blunt, to say profound words of love. She simply did loving things.

Love for her, maybe for her generation, meant service. You showed people your love by serving them. Beginning at five in the morning.

Service expressed itself early in my mom's life. She once told me her goal as a little girl was to be a grandmother by the time she was thirty-nine. As a twelve-year-old she would find little urchins wandering around the neighborhood and take them home and give them a bath and a snack and then send them on their way. She was practicing for having three boys.

And the snacks continued. Food was an important way of showing love. Not big, formal meals with lots of silverware and glasses—that was more my paternal grandmother's way. No it was the small, edible smackeral that brought tiny packets of pleasure: oatmeal and cinnamon toast, grilled sourdough bread dripping with butter and jam, dishes of ice cream that my dad bought by the slab.

And she often insisted on bringing it to you, frequently on a tray. Later it bothered the daughters-in-law to no end to see her repeatedly bring trays of food, saltshaker included, to my father while he watched television. Big-bellied with a remote control in hand, he didn't deserve such pampering, but the ruts of service were worn too deep to turn another way now.

The ruts are still there. My mother is the roving dorm mother of the care facility she lives in. (I don't like the bureaucratic term "care facility," but it beats the obscene euphemism "rest home"—you think they're resting in there?) She is constantly checking in on the neglected, sometimes more often than they want to be checked in on. She goes uninvited into other people's rooms while they're napping and makes sure the blankets are smooth and up to their chins. She sits down next to a mute old man and carries on a one-sided conversation, sure he is better for the chat.

Sometimes it gets her into trouble. She'll tow her roommate, Alma, to the nurse's station, claiming Alma hasn't gotten her pills. The nurse assures my mother that Alma did, in fact, get her pills just twenty minutes earlier. My mother gets in a huff. "I've been with her for the last two hours and you did not give Alma her pills." The nurse is thirty something, but to my mother she is just another sixth grader on the playground who needs a firm voice and a stern look.

Alma is my mother's salvation (forgive me, Jesus). She is one of the locals, having grown up ten miles up the road in a small cluster of decaying houses that the highway signs still pretend is a town. I drove my mom up there once to pass the time during one of my visits. We turned off from the highway and went for a few minutes down a dirt road. My mom remarked on a cluster of cows we passed. We turned around a mile later and came back. She perked up.

"Look," she said, "at those cows, son."

"Yes, Mom. Cows."

Alma wears a jet-black curly wig that always has a pencil stuck in it. She has clown-sized red rouge dots on each cheek. Her perpetual question, "And how are you doing today?" is the opening salvo of a conversation that will circle back, after a few minutes, to a question: "And how are you doing today?"

Though she too often smells of urine, I am glad when Alma is in the room with us. She helps keep the conversation going, playing Laurel to my mom's Hardy. The last time I was there the three of us sat in their room, formerly a hospital maternity room (once a place for the new coming ones, now a place for the old departing ones—life is a circle).

For some reason the name of a hymn comes up. I start to sing it, thinking only to croak out a few bars. But my mother looks at me with a smile and picks up the tune. She is harmonizing underneath my broken melody. She used to do the same with my father, sometimes in church, her sitting at the piano—he the handsome preacher, she the dutiful pastor's wife. Singing for the ladies—and for the gentlemen.

Her voice is tremulous, partly from habit—a traditional way of hymn singing, I think—and partly from age. My memory of the words runs dry—dry, that is, until the words are needed. From somewhere deep inside me comes the words just in time for the next phrase. "There shall be showers of blessing; this is the promise of love." What's next? "There shall be seasons refreshing. Sent from . . ." My mother finishes "the savior above."

151

It is a sweet moment. Singing with my mom. Something I haven't done since I was a child. I don't look at her as we sing, for fear I might cry.

"Showers of blessing," we continue. "Showers of blessing we need." That's certainly true, Mom. We do need them. How can I, given how you are now—and how I am—be a blessing to you? What can I do that will last for more than a few moments?

"Mercy drops round us are falling." Alma has joined in on the refrain. "But for the showers we plead." Maybe that's the most I can hope to do for you, Mom—mercy drops. A call here, a visit there, a book of beautiful photographs that might, if you remember to look at them, take you briefly to other places. The doctors say you can only get worse, steadily and inexorably, as surely as winter follows fall. But even in winter, perhaps, there can be mercy drops.

Singing the hymn awakens the musician in Alma. She reaches under her bed and drags out a large music case. She snaps open the locks to reveal an accordion, and on top of the accordion another wig—perhaps her performance wig.

"I was in five bands, you know."

She lifts the accordion and slides her arms through the straps.

"I played the piano, guitar, drums, and saxophone. I was in seven different bands, you know."

She reaches for a battered notebook that has page after page of song titles scribbled in pencil. No music, just titles.

"I know 850 tunes by heart. Want to hear one?"

Sure I want to hear one, Alma.

Suddenly the room is engulfed in a blast of music. The Beer Barrel Polka. My mom is all smiles. She looks at me and nods, proud of her roommate as she was once proud of me for bringing home a good report card. She starts rhythmic clapping and beams out encouragement to Alma. You go, Alma, I want to say. You go, Mom.

It's not easy to come up with new outings in a town that found its one traffic light underused and took it out. Her favorite place is Southside, a gas station and food mart that also rents videos and sells American flags, hot dogs, pizza slices, and, best of all, ice cream cones. Anytime we're out I can count on a good response when I ask if she'd like some ice cream.

"Ooh, I've just been so hungry for some ice cream, lately. I haven't had ice cream for the longest time."

Or sometimes we go to the park, across from the town swimming pool. She scared me once by plumping herself down in a swing and starting to pump herself up in a big swinging arc, like she was twelve again. I hustled over and slowed her down, unsettled by the look of wild delight in her eyes.

Sometimes we go to the cemetery on the edge of town. We walk among the yew trees and the headstones, she calling out the dates like a sideshow barker.

"Oh, look here. 1826–1887. That's an old one."

Yes, Mom, an old one. What, I think to myself, will your numbers be? What will mine?

As much as I want to focus on my mom during these visits, I can't help but wonder if I am seeing myself—seeing my own future. Her own mother in her last days used to jump out of her bedroom window in her nightgown and run down to the river. And her sister died a few years ago at ninety, a woman no longer acquainted with her own mind. Her father, too. My doctor assures me there is no direct genetic link in these things, only tendencies. I take comfort in my dad's mother being feisty and controlling to the end. I count on science to put an end to all this before my turn comes, but then I counted on science to cure baldness, too.

I suppose in some ways it's worse for the family than it is for the one afflicted. You could argue she's happier now than she was living with my father after the kids had left. That can't have been pleasant, living with a man raised as an only child who was still an only child of sorts, a man who expected to be served but didn't respect the server. She sees her place now, Evergreen, as her home, and home has always been important to her.

Maybe she learned to value home because she was never in one for long. We lived in close to twenty different places just in my time, more before and after—houses, apartments, relative's homes—mostly rented, sometimes bought—one sold after a year before the bank reclaimed it. My father would walk in the door and announce we were moving, sometimes to a different neighborhood, usually to a different town. Often he already had a job there and he went on ahead, leaving my mom to pack everything up and follow. At least that's what my mom says. Maybe it isn't fair to my dad.

So my mother developed the gift of creating an instant feeling of home. Maybe it's why we held on to old furniture so long. Perhaps it made her feel at home no matter what the new walls said. Home was coziness for my mom. She would do small things to make even a motel room homey when we traveled, bringing in our own blankets and pillows from the car.

She says to me often, even now, "Do you remember how you used to whisper 'Danny's home' in my ear when you came in late at night?" I'm quite sure I never called myself "Danny" as a teenager, but these days I pretty much go with whatever version of reality my mom's comfortable with at the moment. It's true she did require me to come to the side of her bed whenever I got home and let her know I was in. If she remembers it as "Danny's home," that's fine with me.

So Evergreen—in Ellendale, in North Dakota—is now her home, as surely as the house in the lemon orchard in Ventura, or the white-trash apartment in Sweetwater with the dilapidated screen door and the gully behind where the kids played, or the nice house on Calle Cita that we lived in when, thanks to her teaching, we had made it.

And because Evergreen is her home, she is increasingly anxious not to be away from it too long. "I better be getting back," she now says after a couple of hours away, "they'll be having dinner soon." She's oblivious to the fact that we are having dinner ourselves as she speaks. I'm not sure whether to find this desire to go back discouraging or comforting. She wants desperately to be taken out, she wants desperately to be taken back. It's the desperate part that hurts. Don't be desperate, Mom. I'm here—we're here—to make sure you have nothing to be desperate about ever again.

Then again, at least she still believes she has a home to go back to.

But for how much longer? For how much longer will she tell herself how lucky she is to have a great roommate like Alma, to be back in the dorms, to have children that all love Jesus? That's what I am tempted to get desperate about myself. When is the personality change coming? When will the anxiety come and no longer go? When will she lose sight of the silver lining? When will she grow bitter and silent? At what point will this—condition, let's call it—be worse for her even than it is for us?

And will I still drive ten hours in a day to see her when that time comes?

For now we can still laugh—together with her and amongst the rest of the family. Let's be honest. She is now funny in a way she never was before. She makes cracks about dad and her marriage she would never have let out. She now excels at friendly put-downs. Alma says how much mom and I look alike. Mom looks at me, shows a comedic sense of timing by waiting a beat, then says, "Boy are you lucky."

But she also does funny things—things you're pretty sure you shouldn't laugh at. But you laugh anyway, considering the alternative.

Like the Christmas at my brother's house where she had a present in a gift bag, which she opened with much exclamation. Then she placed the bag by her chair and watched as the gift opening went around the circle. When it was her turn again, she reached down for the same gift bag and opened it again and again expressed surprise and delight. Once more around the circle and then she opened it for the third time, more surprised and delighted than ever, before someone had the good sense to put the bag somewhere else.

We all laugh at the telling of it, hoping that we are laughing at her condition, not at her, but knowing that sad laughter is sometimes the only way to cope. Because, you see, we, too, have to figure out how to get through this.

If that sounds harsh or selfish, I don't mean it to be. One shouldn't have to "get through" the end of a good life. The last years should be a culmination, not a disintegration, a time of peace and passing on legacies, not a return to the infantile. It should be a time of being a blessing and feeling blessed. That's how it ought to be.

And then there is how it, in fact, is. At least with my mom, and with so many. With each visit she is slightly blanker, slightly less aware, slightly more confused. It cannot be any other way we are told. We should be happy about the "slightly" part.

When I come into her room on visits now, she does not know for sure it is me, her second son, but she does know it is someone special, someone she should give a big greeting to until she gets more clues. She can still name her sons, she just isn't positive which one is standing in front of her. Maybe I should be glad, in this moment, for that much. Maybe I should be glad, in this moment, that she still laughs, that she still tells and understands jokes, that she still is excited about ice cream cones at the gas station.

Tomorrow she will not know me at all. The day after she will not know anyone. The day after that she will be gone. But today, in this moment, she is glad I am here. She smiles and we make small talk and she holds my hand and I take her places. All is right with the world in this moment. When I leave for the five-hour return drive, she will forget before I reach the edge of town that I have been here. But it will not have been for nothing. It will not have been a meaningless visit. For in this moment we are together. Once again "Danny's home" and all is right with the world.

Mercy drops.

An Analysis

It is not appealing to analyze a story from my own life. I'd prefer that it just stand on its own, having whatever effect it will have. But I have asked you to be analytical about your stories, and so I will offer a few brief observations, in hopes that it will be helpful.

Clearly this is a story that centers on a character. It has events, of course, but no clear plot that runs from beginning to end. It does not try to cover my mother's entire life, nor does it start when she is young or even in middle age. Rather it presents a slice of her present, making frequent trips to the past.

Alternating between the present and the past is common in storytelling and in life writing. Doing so exploits our belief that, as William Wordsworth said two hundred years ago, "The Child is Father to the Man." That is, our present is, to a great extent, the product of our past. Stylistically, this approach frees us from the tyranny of the clock and the calendar. I can range anywhere I want in my mother's past to help tell the story of her present. Time, for once, is at my command.

There are supporting characters in this story, including me. I am not crucial to it in one sense. It could be told in third person without changing the picture that emerges of my mom. However, the whole story is told in my voice. I am the one choosing what to highlight, what to pass over. So, of course, it is my story as much as my mother's.

Or maybe more. Because at the same time that I want to preserve something about the character of my mother and her life, this is also a story about my struggle to deal with my mother losing her mind. It is as much about my present relationship with her, and her painful situation, as it is about the kind of person she has been. Life stories are like this—they do many things at once.

On the level of technique, I am trying to do here what I have advised you to do. I gave a lot of thought to the opening sentence in order to draw a reader in as quickly as possible (spending perhaps too much time debating between "I tell my mother lies" and "I tell lies to my mother"). I organize the story around many short scenes from the present and the past. I include dialogue to let us hear the characters speak. I try to establish the settings. I mix reflection with description but try to allow the action to carry the story. I seek out strong verbs and use metaphor and other figurative language as skillfully as I can. In short, I gave more attention to the literary style of the story than I think advisable for most people.

I have claimed that a distinguishing characteristic of legacy work is that it is done for the benefit of others. For whom did I write about lying to my mother? For many people, as I think about it. I wrote it for my mother, because I think she is a remarkable woman whose life of selfless service deserves preserving. I wrote it for my children—and their children—so they would know more about the woman whom they

157

have experienced too little in their lives. And so they would learn some important truths from her. And, without planning to, I also wrote it for you—that is, for anyone else who might read the story, learn from it, and be helped by it. I have already heard from people I do not know who have found it helpful.

But, of course, I also wrote this story for myself. In exploring my mother's present and past, I came to conclusions about how I can reconcile myself to slowly losing her and what I should do. I was unclear about my part in my mom's life when I started writing, and more clear by the time I finished. This illustrates the important truth that when we do legacy work we do not just tell, we discover.

There is nothing wrong with writing for yourself at the same time that you are writing for others. The blessing of legacy work falls widely, and it also falls on you.

Dealing with Pain

This story raises important issues regarding dealing with pain and painful people. There are various kinds and levels of pain in it—my mother's, my father's, my own. Pain is a universal fact of life, and one cannot go deeply into spiritual legacy work without addressing it.

My first rule when advising people about writing about painful things is, "Don't do it if it is likely to cause you harm." Freudian analysis has never proved that uncovering wounds automatically (or even likely) leads to healing them. Some wounds are so profound and so complex that cavalierly telling people to write about them is like beating a hornet's nest with a stick. Telling the story may very well be beneficial, but it should be in the context of receiving help from people who know what they are doing.

My second rule is, "Tell as much or as little as seems right to you." As Denis Ledoux observes, life writing requires you to be neither "an exhibitionist nor a masochist." *You* are in charge of your own stories. Tell as much as you want to tell without feeling pressure to tell everything. Hemingway claimed that "the dignity of movement of an iceberg is due to only one-eighth of it being above water." Sometimes stories are more powerful when you describe the part of the iceberg that can be seen and merely imply the rest.

My third rule is, "Write about what you can now, realizing that you can say more later if you wish." No single story is the definitive telling of any experience. You can write about pain now in the way that seems best now. Then you can write about it more fully later—or not.

And then there is my last rule: "If you can't write about it honestly at this point, then don't write about it at all." It is better to leave a story untold than to offer a whitewashed version of it that doesn't tell the truth. There is no shame in not telling everything about one's life. Some people call it discretion.

Along with the question of *whether* to write, there is the practical issue of *how* to write about painful matters. Briefly, err on the side of underwriting rather than overwriting. Control the tone. A factual, reporting-style tone is often more powerful than an emotionally heated one. And use scenes more than summary and abstraction. Put us in the scene with description and dialogue and setting. Let the story do the work. Reflect on it as is helpful, but don't neglect allowing us to *experience*, as best you can, what you experienced.

Dealing with Painful People

The pain in our lives is often connected to other people. This raises the question of how one deals in writing with painful people as well as with painful events. The short answer is, *treat them better than they deserve.* The name for this is grace, and it doesn't mean you cannot tell the truth. It simply means that in your writing, as in your life, you need to rise above blaming and bitterness—for your own sake and the sake of your story.

My father was a painful person—especially in the lives of my mother and brothers. He is, at the same time, someone I loved and respected. These realities are not mutually exclusive. In the particular story above, he is the heavy. But I do not wish for him to come across as evil or contemptible—only as flawed and human. The words and vignettes I shared may have failed to convey this.

At *the same time* that we are writing honestly, we should also write fairly and even with sympathy, including about characters who have hurt

159

us, knowing that we also have been a source of pain in other people's lives. If you want to be treated with compassion by those you have hurt, you ought to do the same with those who have hurt you—including in your writing.

Interestingly, your sympathy for painful people in your life—at the least recognizing their humanity—leads to the reader's sympathy for you. Readers generally don't want to participate in a mugging of those who cannot speak for themselves.

You can be fair and still tell the truth. Again, the tone of the telling is crucial. Annie Dillard, whom I cited on this topic in chapter 6, says, "I have no grievances left." That is not to say she does not have grief. It suggests however that she is not interested in getting even or in claiming victim status. Which still leaves her free to describe her experience.

Private Writing and Public Reading

Even if one writes fairly, one is still faced with the question of possible fallout from people you know who read what you have written. Especially when writing about family. When I was alone with my computer, writing about my father's infidelities, I felt no particular hesitancy to write the truth. I couldn't tell my mother's story without it, and I had no particular plans necessarily to show it to anyone.

At a later point, however, I decided to try to publish it. Even then, I didn't give much thought to the depiction of my father since he wasn't the central character in the story. When the story was accepted for publication, I thought about it more. The private was now going to be public. Things known only to perhaps a dozen or so people would now be available to anyone who picked up the journal in which it would appear. But I told myself three things—first, my father has been dead for nearly fifteen years; second, my mother has Alzheimer's and would never remember the essay even if I read it to her myself; and, third, no one my parents ever knew would be reading the small-circulation arts journal in which it would appear.

So far, so good. But then someone asked to reprint the story, in a publication affiliated with the university where I was teaching, and I agreed. Now, many people who know me know something unflattering about my father. And I have received a couple of emails from people who knew us both. They express sympathy for me, but also surprise.

I can't help wondering whether I did the right thing.

It seems too melodramatic to ask whether I have *betrayed* my father by writing honestly, but it also feels necessary to ask whether I should have published it. And this is the issue for you too. If you choose to write about painful events and painful people, then write with as much fairness, respect, and even affection as you can muster. But also realize that *you are in control of who reads it and when.* Some stories you can share with everyone, some with only a few, and some you may wait to share until after certain people have died, including yourself.

If you do choose to share your stories now, the happy ones as well as the painful, do not expect universal affirmation, especially from family. Most will be thrilled you preserved a part of your life and theirs. Some will be moved and helped by the stories (which makes any heat you receive worth it). But a few will also quibble, about the details of what you've remembered, the characterization of this person or that, even about the basic facts of what happened. That's okay—smile, don't argue about it, and offer them a snack.

I do not think I betrayed my father by telling part of his story within my mother's. But I have decided I am obligated to write another one— this time focusing on him. This one told the truth, but it didn't tell all of the truth about him. The truths in this story need balancing truths in another story. I need to show him in a fuller light, because if you know *more* about my father, I think you will like him, as I did, even in that period of my youth when I would not have been unhappy to see him dead.

The Ethics of Life Writing

Dealing with painful people raises perhaps the central ethical issue related to life writing. You cannot write at any length about your own life without saying something about someone else's. You are free to say whatever you wish about yourself, but what are the ethical boundaries of what you can say about others?

People have written about this at great length. (I recommend the discussion in chap. 4 of Paul John Eakins's *How Our Lives Become Stories*). Much of it can be boiled down to three categories: accuracy, privacy, and complicity.

Accuracy

I have discussed what constitutes accuracy in life writing earlier, including in the sections on dialogue and on factual truth. Accuracy can be precise when it comes to dates, place names, people present, and the like. But accuracy is more subjective when it comes to characterization, portrayal of motives, telling the whole truth, reflection, and anything relating to meaning or significance.

The best advice, I think, is to be as exact as possible in the first area and as honest as possible in all areas. Readily admit when you are not sure about something, and signal when you are giving your own interpretation of events, not Eternal Truth. At the same time, don't be so apologetic as to be distracting. Readers know you are telling your side of an event, so use "I may be wrong, but . . ." expressions sparingly.

Privacy

The right to privacy is highly valued in our culture. But so, in some areas, is "the public's right to know." We generally think the public has no such right when it comes to the personal life of a nonpublic figure. What are the boundaries?

Many say that the right to privacy ends when a person dies. That certainly was a factor for me when I wrote about my father. But one could just as easily argue that it is even more unfair to speak unfavorably of the dead than the living, because the dead have no chance to answer back. The novelist Philip Roth wonders whether he has violated his father's trust by writing graphically and unsparingly about the indignity of his father's failing body in his last days: "I had dressed him for eternity in the wrong clothes."

I have addressed one set of boundaries above in the discussion of fairness, compassion, and respect, and another with the issue of who gets

162

to read the stories and when. Beyond that, I have come to the conclusion that since no one lives their life in isolation, any part of another's life that is intertwined with mine is as much an aspect of my life as it is of theirs. I have the ethical right to say what I believe is true about their life, and its effect on me, in those areas in which our lives are shared. Shared lives are mutually revealing. To silence someone from speaking of their own life because it does not flatter someone else's is itself unethical.

How I write about them, however, still leaves me morally responsible. The ethics of life writing reside in *how* I tell the story, not *if* I tell it.

Complicity

Readers are also part of this discussion about the ethics of life writing. There is an imprecise line between sharing in others' lives and voyeurism. All art, including storytelling, has an element of inviting an audience into private areas. We read novels, biographies, and confessional memoirs; look at paintings and films originating in private lives; listen to songs that probe intimate personal experience; and the like. And frequently the subject is someone other than the artist.

I don't know exactly where healthy curiosity about someone else's life—the writer's or a person in the writer's life—crosses over into voyeurism, but I think we can usually discern when it happens. When the writing starts to feel unhealthy or vindictive or sensationalistic or masochistic, then reading it feels, to me, unethical. I do not wish to be complicit in someone else's diseased story (which is not the same as a story of disease or woundedness), nor do I want to write in such a way as to make others complicit in mine.

Our culture takes great pleasure in gossip about other people's failures. Spiritual legacy work, with its emphasis on benefiting someone else, has higher aims.

8

So You Hate to Write

Reluctant Writers and Other Forms of Legacy Work

I write when I'm inspired, and I see to it that I'm inspired at nine o'clock every morning.

Peter De Vries

I have argued that everyone can and should tell their stories, particularly in written form, to better stand against the fleetingness of human life. But I am also realistic. Many people, even if convinced of the value, will simply never get around to it. I would like, therefore, to offer some guidance, first, on how to prompt the reluctant to write their stories, and, second, on other forms of spiritual legacy work that do not require you to confront an empty page.

Prompting the Reluctant

Many times people want to preserve *someone else's* stories—or to help that person pass on a part of his or her spiritual legacy. How do you persuade others to preserve, in one form or another, some of their values and wisdom and stories? Often an adult child wants a parent to do some kind of legacy work, and, just as often, the parent is reluctant or feels inadequate to the task. What then?

Here are some practical suggestions:

Emphasize Who Benefits

Many, as we have seen, deflect legacy work because they minimize the importance of their own lives or plead inadequacy to write about it. Older people, especially, are less likely to find their lives fascinating and worth exploration. They may even see talking about themselves as ethically dubious.

To such people you must make it clear that while there are clear benefits for the teller in legacy work, the real beneficiaries are others. Explain that other people *need* their stories and reflections. This is not for entertainment (though it can be very entertaining), nor for stroking one's ego (though it can feel very good to realize the significance of one's stories), but for the good of others.

The most important "others" to many people are their children and their children's children. Appeal to their sense of responsibility and desire to do something helpful (but note the guilt caveat below). Present spiritual legacy work as a gift they can give to their children and a blessing they can give to their grandchildren and beyond.

Sometimes you will find that older people really do want to tell their stories, but simply need a little nudge. The son of a man in one of my life-writing courses took me aside one day and said of his missionary father, "He tells everyone he is only taking your course because the kids are bugging him to write down his stories, but in fact it was his idea from the first and he's really excited about it."

Keep it Low-Key

Few people like pressure, and fewer still respond well to pressure to do something that they actually do not have to do. No one *has* to do spiritual legacy work. Therefore I suggest an approach of low-key

166

persistence. That is, keep the task from seeming too big in the other person's mind, but also do not simply let it slide if nothing is forthcoming.

One way of underplaying the effort required is to indicate that these things are "just for the family," or maybe just for you. And emphasize realistic goals: "I'm not suggesting you write your life story. I'd be happy if you just got a few stories down, or if you just wrote something short on what you think is important in life. Something the grandkids can have once you're gone—and something *their* kids will have."

Avoid guilt trips, however. Guilt trips are usually trips to nowhere and back. Help others see the value of spiritual legacy work and then stand back. More often than not, if they understand its value, they will want more than anyone else to tell what has happened to them and what they make of it.

At the same time that one is low-key, one should also be persistent. People will often pass off first requests for anything they are not already inclined to do. If a couple of tries produces no results, then see if offering to help, as described below, loosens the logjam.

Start Small

If writing down stories seems like too much to those you are helping, try starting them with a spiritual will (chap. 2), which can be as short as a paragraph or two. Explain to them what it is and show them some examples. Maybe show them one you have written yourself, and then make clear how much you would value something like this from them.

If they confess to drawing a blank on where to start, offer them some prompts. Adapt some of the questions from the "Spiritual Legacy Questions" in the appendix. Remember the importance of "writing before you write" as discussed in chapter 6.

If they do a spiritual will, wait a bit (five minutes to five months) and then ask them *why* they said what they did. That is, ask them to tell the stories behind this or that in the spiritual will. And when they tell or refer in passing to a story, ask them to write that story down. That is, move them from a statement of values and convictions to the stories out of which they arise.

Provide Some Help

Use some of the ideas from this book to create raw material to work with. Encourage prewriting such as lists of stories, characters, or values. (You can create partial lists yourself for them, requesting favorite stories you have heard them tell orally.) Maybe lead them through an exercise or two, writing along with them if that helps, but leaving them alone to do it if your hovering is bothersome.

Make a list of story prompts, asking your loved one to tell stories about specific events or people. Instead of, "Write about when you were young," say, "Write about the time your horse got stuck in the mud." See some of the prompts and questions in the appendix. Give them a written list of prompts, something they can look at on their own time when you're not around.

Discern how big of an obstacle the "writing" aspect of all this is. My father did not write personal letters. He simply wasn't comfortable in front of a blank piece of paper, and I don't think he would have written down stories had I asked before he unexpectedly died (which I greatly regret I did not). He was the central storyteller of my life, but he was banking on me to get them down on paper.

If the act of writing is a significant obstacle, then consider other approaches, as discussed below. Perhaps use a recording device into which they can tell stories or talk about values. You or someone else can transcribe the recording later. Be aware that some people, and some cultures, do not respond well to a machine capturing their words. You can also hire a professional (also see below) who has experience interviewing others, getting good stories, and writing them up.

Check In

The persistent part of the "low-key but persistent" approach means that you check in with your would-be writers occasionally to see what's percolating. Not every time you see them, or they'll stop answering the door. But maybe every four to six weeks. If they are open to it, perhaps work out a writing schedule for them (see chap. 4). Identify good days for them to do some spiritual legacy work and have them write it on their calendar.

Write Some of the Story Yourself

If worse comes to worst, and nothing is working, write down one of their stories yourself. Obviously, it will have to be one you have already heard them tell. Better to preserve stories filtered through someone else (in this case, you) than not to preserve them at all.

Show the story or stories to the person you want to be working on their spiritual legacy. Maybe even ask them for details while you are writing. Perhaps intentionally make it incomplete or fragmented, which might prompt them to take the story over and do it correctly. My father once read a story I told in print about him and said, "If you'd asked, I could have made it better." It was an appropriate rebuke, but I should have said, "Maybe you ought to write them down yourself so they get told right."

INTERVIEWING

If you are going to write part or all of someone else's story, you may need to interview them. Interviewing well is a skill, but a few pointers are enough to make anyone at least minimally able to perform one.

The goals of an interview are first, to generate useful information, and, second, to spark interest in the person being interviewed in preserving his or her stories. A third goal is to get actual words from the speaker that can be used in the piece itself, so that it contains his or her own voice.

A single word sums up what an interviewer needs to do: prepare. Preparation includes establishing for yourself the *goal* of an interview. What, specifically, do you want to learn? Before the interview, learn as many basic *facts* as you can about the person and the specific story you are pursuing. Knowing facts in advance will help you generate good questions. Give thought also to *where* an interview should take place and how you are going to *record* it. Both are important for putting the interviewee at ease.

Finally, you should *prepare a list of questions* in advance. Talking to others first may help you in this. You do not have to write down every question, but you should have at least a few to start the discussion off. Listening closely to answers, following up promising leads, and being willing to explore unexpected territory is crucial. Do not simply ask the next question on your list, nor feel you have to ask all the questions you have prepared.

Some of your questions may be factual (especially initially as you warm the subject up), but the most important ones will be open-ended, inviting longer, even rambling answers. Encourage the elements of story-telling—ask them to describe, to create the scene, to tell what someone actually said. Gently push them toward specifics. Don't talk too much yourself. When you are nearly finished, ask them if there is something they want to add that you haven't asked about.

There is more to say about interviewing, but this is enough to start with. Remember, however, that even the most successful interview only produces raw material. You still have the challenges of deciding what parts to use and of shaping it into a successful story.

RESEARCH

Whether writing a story yourself, or helping someone else write his or hers, you will sometimes need to track down information. So telling a story will at times begin with research. Sources for information include talking to other people, letters, diaries or journals, newspaper articles, books, timelines, databases, the internet. Sometimes you will want to correct a person's memory (the dates of a battle, year of a wedding, location of an event, name of a person), and sometimes you won't (how they remember something is often more important than petty details).

Specialty books and internet sites have been created to help identify a wide variety of public events by year (see "Resources" in the appendix). Starting with these can itself sometimes prompt a story (for instance, the year a favorite song was number one).

Be Glad for What You Get

When you get any form of spiritual legacy work from someone, receive it warmly and gratefully, no matter how limited or fragmentary it may be. Whether you get a two-paragraph spiritual will or a single written story, you have gotten more than most ever do. Play it by ear as to whether and when you might ask for more. You don't want to seem greedy or dissatisfied with what you've received.

The hope is that having people doing a bit of their spiritual legacy will light a fire. Get some people going on this kind of work and you better clean your reading glasses because you're going to get a lot of big envelopes in the mail. They discover the value and pleasure of probing their own lives and the stories begin to flow like the Mississippi.

Others will make an initial effort and that's it. Again, be thankful for whatever you receive. And if it doesn't feel like enough, then commit to not making the same mistake yourself and get to work on passing on your own stories.

Telling Someone Else's Stories

I have suggested that one tactic for getting reluctant writers to preserve stories is to start writing their story yourself. If you are lucky, they will take over and put you out of a job. But sometimes that person—like my father—is dead, or (like my mother) incapable of remembering. If my father's and mother's stories are going to last, my brothers or I will to have to tell them.

In situations like ours, one can do all the preliminary work of list making and freewriting for their stories that I have advised you to do for your own. But when it comes to actually writing any particular story, some choices have to be made.

What Grammatical Person

The first choice is what grammatical person to tell the story in. You can write in third person, the most common approach in storytelling, using *he* and *she*. Or you can write in first person, the most common approach in memoir writing, using *I* and *we*. The reader gets a different feel from "Darrell Taylor had his second child when he was twenty-five" than from "My father was twenty-five when I was born."

There are pluses and minuses to each approach. The first person is more intimate, mimicking the sense of closeness created when one person

171

shares a part of his or her life directly with another. It can also sound more authoritative, given our natural inclination to attribute truthfulness to someone telling us a story about his or her own life. But first person can be hard enough to sustain in fiction, and is even more challenging when writing biographically (as opposed to autobiographically). And it may feel inauthentic for you to write as though you were someone else.

Writing in third person feels more natural when telling someone else's story because it is how we pass on second-hand stories in daily life: "Mary said it was the worst haircut she had ever had in her life." It allows you to confess openly when you don't know something or when you are guessing. It also allows you the luxury to reflect and comment on the other person's story. This may be something you want to do, especially if it is the story of someone close to you or if it involves events in which you were involved. If I write about my father, his story is inevitably part of mine, even if I am writing about something that happened before I was born.

Voice

The second choice you have to make when telling someone else's story involves voice. Voice, as we have seen, is the personality and sensibility and unique way of speaking that lies behind how each of us expresses ourselves. You needn't worry much about voice when telling your own stories, because it will come through naturally as part of your habits of expression and how you see your life. But you do need to give it some thought when telling someone else's story.

How much of their actual way of expressing themselves are you going to try to preserve in telling their story? If you use first person, you are going to have to preserve a lot. In fact, you need to tell the story as closely as you can remember to how they told the story, using their characteristic expressions and verbal tics and way of conveying events. Otherwise it won't sound like them, and the "I" will seem manufactured.

But even if you use third person, you need to get as much of their own voice into the story as possible. The single best way of doing so is to include dialogue, as discussed above and in chapter 6. When we hear their actual words in their own story, we will feel to some degree as though they are telling us the story themselves. We will actually hear two voices, yours as the conveyer of the story and the voice of the person whose story is being told. And that is perfectly fine. Most stories are, ultimately, stories within a story anyway.

These choices you make when telling someone else's stories are more aesthetic than ethical. If you use first person, you may want to begin with something like, "My father used to tell the following story, as best as I can remember. . . ." The story will not be 100 percent accurate, any more than a photograph is, but it will put into lasting form something that should not be lost.

Other Forms of Spiritual Legacy Work

This book emphasizes two primary forms for preserving a spiritual legacy—spiritual wills and story legacies. There are, of course, many other forms, a few of which I will briefly describe below. Most of them are related to telling a story, some more directly than others.

If you do an internet search using any of the following terms, you will find a whole universe of websites, discussion boards, individual practitioners, articles, and affinity groups for further exploration. (Check "Resources" in the back of the book for some specific recommendations.)

Memoir, Life Writing, Ethical Will Instructors, and Workshops

Many individuals, and some organizations, provide help in writing about your life, in constructing what is variously called an ethical will, spiritual-ethical will, or legacy letter, and in generally helping you create some kind of legacy. You can find workshops or receive one-on-one help. Some will provide guidance for your own writing, and others will do the writing for you.

This kind of work often involves values-identification exercises, guided writing, directed oral storytelling (sometimes recorded), and the like. It can also include guidance on how to put one's writing into print (usually self-published—see next chapter) for distribution to family members and friends.

Personal Historians

While many professionals offer help in various kind of legacy work, there is a specialized group called personal historians who make this work their calling. They have a national organization called the Association of Personal Historians (APH), and they work primarily with ethical wills and memoirs.

Personal historians conduct interviews (typically ten to twenty hours worth), do family research, write a history, organize photographs, and create a printed and bound final product for distribution. Personal historians do the writing themselves, rather than leading you in your own writing. Some also work with video and audio recording.

Audio Memoir

Some legacy work focuses on audio memoirs, producing digital recordings of people talking about their lives and telling their stories. Recording sessions are preceded by exercises designed to prime and focus the speaker's thinking. Multiple speakers can be included on a single digital recording. Recordings are edited and sequenced, and music and narration can be added, so that the final product sounds polished, not rambling. Photos can be used on the covers of the final product.

Videography

Videography adds the visual element to those features of an audio memoir just described. It too can use music and narration, as well as the speaker's own voice. It also can do a lot with photographs, creating a documentary (yet intimate) feel around a person speaking from his or her own life. The final product is a digital recording that can be mass-produced and distributed.

Journals, Daybooks, and Diaries

Journaling is an ancient form of legacy work, and the topic of many books. It differs from spiritual wills and story legacies in that it tends to be highly personal, fragmented, and usually not for sharing with

174

others. Because journaling often focuses on values and reflections, and contains the seeds of many stories, journals and diaries can be a rich source of raw material for legacy work intended for the benefit of others.

Writers use daybooks much as artists use sketchpads. They record observations, try out descriptions, play with language, work out plot and storylines, and otherwise create material that may someday see its way into a piece of writing.

The disadvantage of journaling for spiritual legacy purposes is that they tend not to tell complete stories, and they are often so focused on the present that they do not adequately explore the past. But they can be a good resource for life writing.

Blogging

The quickest way to inform the world about your life is through tweeting and blogging. Never has so much information about the details of so many lives been offered in so many public places for instantaneous consumption (and heartburn). Some of it could pass for spiritual legacy work if it focuses on a life and on passing wisdom from that life to others.

Blogging has the advantages of requiring little effort beyond sitting at a keyboard and of providing instant availability to others. One disadvantage of blogs for spiritual legacy work is that they exist only digitally unless transferred to something more permanent. Further, it is difficult to target a blog to any one individual or group, a main goal of this work. Blogging could be a place to try out ideas and perhaps get feedback before moving them to more lasting forms.

A disadvantage of using personal historians and audio and video approaches is that they tend to capture a limited number of stories and values. They are much better than nothing—and can be very powerful—but a few hours of talking will only skim the surface of a lifetime of living. Someone writing over time from an ever-expanding story list will pass on much more. But for people who are likely never to write anything down at all, these other approaches are attractive. Of course they also cost money.

Visual Approaches: Life Maps, Collages, and Annotated Photographs

In chapter 4 we discussed the use of visual elements (from drawings to photographs) to both create raw material for writing and enhance the finished product. It is possible to make these primary rather than supportive. *Life maps* use symbols (for example, a dollar sign, diploma, trophy, broken heart), simple drawings, images from magazines, photographs, and other symbolic or tangible objects and arrange them so that they relate together in a meaningful way. Usually they include labels and annotations, and occasionally a timeline (not necessarily linear). Lines or paths are often drawn between different items to show relationships (for example, a line connecting a drawing of a friend's face with a symbol for the job where you first met). They are best used to clarify things for the creator and as prompts for writing, but they can also stand alone.

A *collage* is an artistic arrangement of various disparate elements (for example, paint, newspaper clippings, letters or lettering, objects) brought together to form an aesthetic whole. If used for autobiographical purposes, the elements are somehow connected to the creator's life. The result can be powerful but often requires explanation and elaboration for a viewer who does not know its creator well.

We discussed the use of photographs as prompts for writing and supplements to spiritual wills or story collections in chapter 4. One could use photographs alone as a spiritual legacy, but they would need both conscious arrangement and some kind of annotation to be effective as a spiritual legacy.

Scrapbooking

Scrapbooking is a world unto itself; its practitioners are passionate and legion. There are a wide variety of approaches to scrapbooking, but the common denominator is the collection and arrangement of artifacts that are tied to a memory and that prompt stories. A strength of scrapbooking for legacy work is its tangibility. Rather than abstractions and generalizations, one has physical objects from the real world that are part of the history of a life lived.

Scrapbooks offer a kind of narrative of a life or an event or an on-going interest in something. A possible weakness of scrapbooking for legacy work is that scrapbooks tend to require a narrator to be present. Viewing someone else's scrapbook can be puzzling at best if that person is not there to tell the story behind each item.

One way of overcoming that difficulty is to include writing as part of the scrapbook. Along with the physical artifacts, one can insert written or recorded accounts of the stories behind them.

Memory Boxes

Memory boxes, sometimes called wisdom boxes, are related to scrap-booking but presented in the form of a shallow box for display. The box can contain anything its creator desires, including photographs and booklets of stories, reflections, a spiritual will, or a journal. It usually contains artifacts as well, including three-dimensional ones that do not fit so well in the pages of the typical scrapbook (for example, a class ring, stuffed animal, or charm bracelet).

Memory boxes can remain in the possession of their creators or can be given as a legacy gift to others.

Quilting

Women have been telling stories in quilts and other crafts for centuries. Sometimes the story is hidden in a pattern or even a stitch, and sometimes it is more accessible in a symbol or design. The movement to use quilts to commemorate the stories of AIDS victims, beginning at the end of the last century, is a contemporary twist on this old tradition.

Patterns and symbols do not give us the details of a story or a life, but they can at least provide a sketch of the arc of a life and lead to conversations and storytelling. Some quilters now use new technologies to transfer photos, documents (such as birth certificates or wedding programs), and even typescript (poems, vows, Scripture passages, spiritual wills) onto fabric. These are used to create quilts or wall hangings that speak clearly of a specific life.

Family Meeting Facilitators

Whereas many life-writing professionals work with individuals or a few family members, some work with extended families. They organize family meetings or reunions with an emphasis on doing legacy work. They guide nuclear or extended families in reflection, values clarification, story preservation, and planning for the future.

Sometimes these meetings arise at particular times of need—planning what to do with aging parents, the transfer of estates, or relationship crises, for example. There are specialized versions of family legacy work that focus on specific relationships, such as between a husband and wife or between grandparents and grandkids.

Many times this kind of work emphasizes communication between the generations, so that the younger learn from the older and the older hear the perspectives of the younger. There may be a written finished product, or people may simply go away having shared their lives and heard important stories and perspectives.

Life Coaching

Life coaching is a relatively new development in the ancient practice of mentoring and guiding that aims to help individuals and organizations establish and achieve specific goals. Basically, it addresses the question, "In what ways would you like to improve yourself or your life, and how can we make that happen?" There are many different foci and approaches to life coaching, but one of them is legacy related.

Life coaches who specialize in legacy work offer one-on-one or group training in values identification, goal setting, written and financial legacy creation, and the like. They can offer direction in journaling, memoir writing, communication between the generations, spiritual reflection, retirement planning with an emphasis on values, and other activities related to spiritual legacy.

Estate Planning with a Legacy Emphasis

Among the many professionals who help with estate planning are those who include an emphasis on legacy matters that go beyond the financial. They direct clients in reflecting on what they want their legacy to be in the larger sense.

Some guide clients through the creation of an ethical or spiritual will or similar document, with an emphasis on leaving a record of their core values and insights for future generations. They may emphasize family-wide estate and legacy planning as well as planning for individuals or couples. Some estate planners will arrange for the writing of family or business histories.

Charitable Giving

One of the clearest ways we enact our core values is by how we spend and give away our money. Charitable-giving counselors can help indentify and focus giving opportunities in ways that become part of your larger legacy—spiritual as well as financial. Giving wisely requires the kind of values identification, reflection, and other legacy-related activities we have discussed. Charitable giving creates and supports institutions that have stories that reflect the values and vision of their founders and sustainers.

Family and Organizational Legacies

Everything that can be done by and for an individual can be done for an entire family, organization, or business. Organizations have a story, often a compelling one. Many businesses are actually selling a story when they promote their products. And the collective story of a family over generations is different from the personal stories of individual members. Most professionals in the legacy field can adapt their services to any scale.

Software and Other Aids

We are a "do-it-yourself" culture, and there are many aids to doing spiritual legacy work on your own (this book being one). Search the internet using any of the terms that recur in this book—*memoir, ethical will, life story, legacy, personal historian, journaling, life coaching, life*

179

maps, scrapbooking, and the like—and you will find books, merchandise, individuals, and organizations related to spiritual legacy work.

Take those same words and pair them in a search with the word *software* and you will find computer software that will guide you in doing specific kinds of legacy work. Using any external aid, whether another person or computer software, can help provide direction and motivation that moves you from thinking about a spiritual legacy to actually creating one.

9

What to Do
with Spiritual Legacy Work

Revising, Preserving, and Sharing

If you've heard this story before, don't stop me, because I'd like to hear it again.

Groucho Marx

The future belongs to those who give the next generation reason for hope.

Pierre Teilhard de Chardin

All right. So you have written a story—or twenty stories. What do you do now?

The first thing you do is work on the story to make it more effective. The second is determine the best form to preserve it in. And the third is consider who to share it with and how. In sum, the next steps after getting a story down on paper are revising, preserving, and sharing.

Writing a first draft is like giving birth—it's unpredictable and messy. The baby is beautiful but bloody and upset. These next steps are like cleaning the baby up, wrapping it in a warm blanket, and offering the contented newborn to visitors to admire and hold.

Revising

Because it may smell like schoolwork, revising strikes some people as the least attractive part of telling their stories, but it is often what distinguishes a pretty good story from a really good story. It is especially important if you follow the advice to just get a story down on paper initially without much thought for form, word choice, grammar, paragraphing, or punctuation. What you have now is a bloody, squalling newborn.

When you revise you are using a different part of your brain than you used initially in writing the story. You move from being an author who has been engaged in the imaginative act of remembering and telling to being an editor who is engaged in the more objective act of analyzing and evaluating. Here are some guidelines as you edit and revise.

Levels of Revision: Moving from Larger to Smaller

Revise means literally to "look again." You are re-visioning the story (or spiritual will) you have in front of you and comparing it with the original "vision" you had for it. Does the story do what you had hoped? If not, does it do something else that you are happy about? In either case, what can be done to make it even more effective?

Revision at this level is *not* simply looking for mistakes. It is asking big questions about the story, the answers to which will guide how to make the story better. One doesn't revise in order to make a story more correct, but to make it more effective.

Here are some of the questions you can ask about your story's overall *conception*:

A. What was I trying to accomplish in the first place?
　—does this story succeed in doing that?

—if not, am I happy with what it does instead?

—if not, what, *specifically*, is keeping it from succeeding?

B. What related material could helpfully be added?

C. What unhelpful material could be deleted and possibly saved for another story?

D. What would readers have trouble understanding or picturing or relating to here? How can I help? Where am I not giving them enough information?

E. What does the story need more of?

F. What does the story need less of?

G. What are the strongest parts of the present draft?

H. What are the weakest parts of the present draft?

I. Where are the "energy drains" where the story lags? Are there sections that are repetitious, filler, marking time, or tedious?

J. What has promise but needs more development or better expression?

After asking and addressing these large-scale questions, one can move to the level of *execution*. Here you deal with questions of how effectively you have executed or put into practice the specific aspects of your story that combine to make it realize its larger vision. You can ask the following:

A. Is the story built around a scene or scenes?

B. Is enough attention paid to setting? Does the reader know where and when the story is taking place?

C. Does the story have a strong character at the center? Is that character adequately described?

D. Does it reveal human nature? Does it show the motivations for why people do what they do?

E. Does anything *happen* in the piece—either an external or internal action? Is there a sense of an event or plot unfolding, or a sense of development, as opposed to a feeling of stasis or inertia?

F. Is there something at stake? Does the reader feel a sense of conflict or pressure or something that needs to be resolved?

G. Am I both describing well *and* reflecting on what I am describing? That is, do I both show and tell?

H. Does the story open strong? Create immediate interest?

 I. Does it conclude satisfactorily (and not just stop)? Is there a sense of completion? An effective last sentence?

 J. Is each phase of the story adequately developed before I move on to the next? Does the story seem to have a beginning, middle, and end?

K. Does the story try to do too many things at once, giving a sense of no one thing being treated sufficiently?

L. Do all the details contribute to the overall effect I want to create?

M. Have I kept my promises? That is, if I raise an issue or arouse curiosity about something, do I offer adequate resolution by the story's end?

Only after addressing larger issues of conception and execution does one get to the level of specific paragraphs, sentences, and words. Here you address questions of *expression*—the details of wording, grammar, and punctuation. Even here one should not simply look for errors, but for opportunities. Where can something, even if it is correct, be made more effective? Here are some questions to ask:

A. Am I describing in an interesting way that invites the reader into the scene?

B. Are the details significant and revealing or merely piled up?

C. Is it always clear where each part of the story is in space and time?

D. Is it clear who is talking?

E. Is dialogue used effectively and punctuated correctly?

 F. Where are the clichés? How can I replace clichés with something more interesting?

G. Where am I wordy? Where can I cut out excess words and sentences?

H. Am I choosing interesting words? Am I making use of figurative language? Does the wording sound natural and realistic rather than strained or "literary" or artificial (often the result of trying too hard to write impressively)?

I. Where am I unclear (at any level)?

J. Are my sentences easily readable? Do they need to be shorter or simplified? Varied in length and rhythm?

K. Do I break the story into helpful paragraphs? Are they usually three to five sentences in length?

L. Do I have helpful transitions between paragraphs and between sections of the story?

M. Do I have a helpful title that provides some direction for the story?

N. Where are there problems of spelling, punctuation, grammar, or typing (what many people think of when they think of revision)?

After one has moved from the large questions of overall conception of the story to the smallest questions of grammar or punctuation, one can return to the largest questions of all. These are the questions of *significance*. I want to emphasize again that not every story you need to tell will have dramatic, life-shaping significance. There is profit simply in telling what it was like to walk to school or about the time you got your first bicycle. But we will want some of our stories to deal with deeper issues, and of those stories we can ask the following:

A. Does the story convey the meaning or significance I intended? Why or why not?

B. Is the significance of the events of this story evident, or would the meaning be deepened by reflection? If so, have I reflected enough within the story? Too much? Are my reflections repetitious—saying the same thing in only slightly different words?

C. Is there a deeper subject beneath the surface subject of the story? Should I let the perceptive reader discover it, or should I make it explicit?

D. Does the story offer insight (not just facts)? Into my life or someone else's life or life in general?

E. Will a reader understand something better (about me or my subject) for having read this?

F. Does the piece have a human feel about it? Have I been afraid to show emotion? Or have I overdone the emotion, not trusting the story itself?

G. Does the piece pass on to the reader some kind of wisdom about life?

H. Do I feel good about what it accomplishes, no matter how modest the intended purpose might have been?

Further Revising Advice

AVOID THE EXTREMES

When reading over your own stories or other spiritual legacy efforts, avoid two extremes. The first extreme is becoming sentimental about your writing and loving it so much that you are unwilling to change a single word. This is, after all, your life you are writing about, and it is natural and advisable to be emotionally invested in it. But you should not be so invested in these particular words that you are unable to see what works and doesn't work, or what changes could make the story even better. It is especially hard to cut things out, because it may feel like you are cutting out a part of your life. But understand that anything you need to cut out to make a story better can itself be its own story at another time.

The second extreme is despairing over your writing. For every person who likes their prose too much, there are ten who do not like it enough. These are often the people who said at the beginning, "I can't tell a story," and now they are likely to say, "See, this is junk and no one would want to read it." There is no junk in spiritual legacy work. Every attempt to pass on something to another is valuable. The value lies not in your innate writing abilities but in the blessing you offer to another life.

So at the revision stage try to be both sympathetic to the telling of your stories and at the same time objective about how you have told it. Read your story as a reader, not as the author, and ask yourself the questions listed above. Improve the story as much as you can, but don't demand more of it than the occasion requires. It may be a very simple story, but it deserves the respect we should give to any human life.

READERS KNOW ONLY WHAT YOU TELL THEM

Stories sometimes fail because the writer assumes, usually unconsciously, that the reader is as familiar with the people and the world the stories describe as the writer is. When you start a story about Uncle Clinton, you have a wealth of memories and impressions and emotions associated with your favorite uncle. The reader may have only a name—Uncle Clinton. So if you launch off into an Uncle Clinton story without providing what we need to see and hear and understand Uncle Clinton, the reader may have only a name doing some things.

In your mind, there is a whole world, but the reader doesn't have access to your mind. If it's not on the page, then it won't be part of the reader's experience. So in revising, ask yourself if you have said enough, described enough, reflected enough for the reader's experience to be close to your memory of the story.

READ OUT LOUD

When revising, or even in composing a first draft, read the story out loud. The ear will hear what the eye does not see. It will tell you when sentences sound awkward or are too long. It will let you know when you are going on too long about a certain topic or when you fail to include enough information. I have read published stories of my own to audiences and heard clunkers that made me wince—undesirable repetitions, missing words that would have clarified something, an awkward rhythm or missed opportunity to use a more interesting word. Better to hear it yourself at the revision stage than to hear it later.

FIND OTHER READERS

It is important at the revision stage to be objective about your own work. But there are limits to how objective you can be about anything you have done, especially if it is something as personal as spiritual legacy work. So look for other readers. A second pair of eyes, especially those of someone who does not know the particulars of your story, can be invaluable.

But choose carefully. As Denis Ledoux says, "Choose people who will critique the work itself rather than you." You need someone who will say,

"I think this part is strong, but the section after it is confusing," not someone who will say, "Wow, you are even more screwed up than I thought," or, "It didn't happen that way at all," or, "I hope mother never sees this."

You need readers who are honest but sympathetic, and who have at least some sense about good writing. (Everyone is a story evaluator by nature. We all do it every day.) Just ask them to tell you what they think works and doesn't work. Have them mark any place where they need more explanation and anywhere they got more explanation than they wanted. You can also provide them with more specific questions, but it is usually better to let them just react generally first, before you direct them to specific issues in the story.

Where do you find such readers? They may be a family member, a friend, a respected acquaintance, or even a professional. There are people who make their living doing freelance editing. They can evaluate a manuscript at every level—from large-scale conceptualization to the minutiae of commas and semicolons. (See below for more on editors.) Wherever you find your readers, remember the admonition above to avoid extremes. Be open enough to consider changes but also confident enough to know that it is your story, not someone else's, and that you are rightfully the final judge.

Don't Revise Too Soon—If at All

Revising, like some desserts, is better served cold. It's best if you can put a story or other spiritual legacy work aside for a while before you revise it—a few days, a few weeks, even a few months. Let the dust and the emotions settle. Pick it up later when it will seem slightly new and foreign even to you. You will then read it more as a reader will someday read it, not as the one who just wrote it. You may find some parts that won't even make sense to you anymore, and that is a helpful thing to discover. But you will also find parts that amaze and move you, as though they were written by someone else with more skill than you ever gave yourself credit for possessing. It will remind you that the power is in the story, not primarily in the storyteller.

But if all this talk about revision scares you away from even starting— if it sounds too much like that disastrous high school English class you took—then forget about revision. Forget about openings and endings, paragraphs and punctuation, description and dialogue, and everything else. Just tell the story. Get it down and pass it on and let the devil take the hindmost. Better a raw story than no story at all.

Organizing Your Stories

Before You Start

As indicated in chapter 3, never say to yourself, much less to anyone else, "I am going to write my life story." It is just too big a project to contemplate. You will be like the donkey standing between two haystacks that starves because it can't decide which stack to eat from first.

Some people, however, want to know where they are heading before they start out. For such people (the kind who lay out the clothes they are going to wear the next day the night before), it is possible to do some planning before writing the first story. I have suggested, for instance, that all aspiring storytellers make lists—of events, characters, and values—and look for where they intersect. If you want to plan ahead, you can look at those lists and select the first three, six, or fifty stories you want to tell and the order you want to tell them in.

You can group stories together by time period or by characters or by topics or by whatever method seems right to you. You can also plan out when you will write each story, assigning it a place on your calendar. Good for you if you can do that (we will also put you in charge of directing the Christmas pageant), but beware of the paralyzing potential of the overly ambitious project. Picking one story off a story list can seem like a pleasant walk in the park. Looking at a plan to tell twenty stories may loom like a marathon.

After You Have Written

The world is better for the telling of even a single story. And perhaps you will only write one—for the benefit of one other person. But storytelling is addictive. Tell one and you are likely to tell another. And that will lead to two or three more. In time, you may find you have written down a lot of stories. What do you do then?

The first thing you do is organize them. Give some thought to a logical, effective order of stories. When poets put their poems into a collection, they do not usually put them in the order in which they were written. They ask which poems mutually illuminate, clarify, and resonate with each other and then put those in proximity to each other. You should do the same with your stories.

Spread your printed stories in front of you, or make a list of their titles. Consider different ways of grouping them. The simplest and most obvious plan is to order your stories chronologically, moving from ancestors to childhood to the present. This is a natural pattern that satisfies our instinctive sense for the movement from beginning to end. It is not without complications, however. Where do you put a story from late in your grandmother's life? Does it come first because she was born before you were, or at the time in your life when you heard it? Even a chronological plan will require decisions.

Another possibility is a topical arrangement. Stories dealing with similar topics can be clustered together. For example, you can group school stories, church stories, work stories, family stories, travel stories, army stories, and funny stories. Topical arrangements are a little more imaginative than pure chronology, though you may have trouble deciding what to do with a story that fits more than one topic or that is the only story on a specific topic. (There's nothing wrong with an "Other Stories" section.)

More complex yet is a thematic arrangement. Perhaps you find you tell a lot of stories around certain values, such as compassion or perseverance. Others may group around faith or faithfulness or prayer. Others may explore the meaning of friendship or love or service. A challenge in arranging thematically is that some stories may not seem to have a theme or they have a theme unlike any of the others. These are stories you can also group together under an "Other Stories" heading.

There are other possibilities. You can organize stories strictly by character—stories about your mother, or your father, siblings, teachers, bosses, friends, and so on. More arbitrarily, you could organize by the length of stories (short ones first, then longer ones), or by what you take to be the quality of the stories (the best ones first, the weaker ones buried in the back), or simply by order of your own enjoyment (the ones you like most first, the rest to follow).

And it is often advisable to use a combination of approaches. You may have a series of chronologically arranged stories, followed by a series of topically and then thematically arranged stories, ending up with an "Odds and Ends" section.

Given how easy it is to manipulate texts digitally, you may even consider having more than one arrangement and producing different versions of your collected stories for different purposes. This could be especially useful if there are some stories you hesitate to make available to everyone. An exceptionally private or painful story, or one that might spark trouble in the family, can be left out of one edition of your stories, but included in the "Complete Works."

Whichever approach you choose, start with one of your strongest stories. You want the first impression to be a good one.

Additional Material

As we have seen, spiritual legacy story collections often contain more than just the stories. Consider an introduction that briefly states why you have written these stories and what your hopes are for them. This can be a general "to the reader" introduction, or it can be directed to the specific person or persons you had in mind when you were writing them.

Photographs can add interest and power. Photographs, as we have seen, can be used as a prompt for writing a story in the first place, in which case it would be very appropriate to include the photograph with the story. But apart from any particular story, photographs can be spread through a collection (or collected in a single place) to serve as visual markers that tell a story in their own right. Consider briefly annotating the photographs.

Also consider including copies of letters (photocopied or typed from the originals), documents (marriage license, report card, résumé), newspaper clippings, drawings, or maps. A timeline can be helpful. A family tree can clarify relationships for the younger generation. A story

191

collection could be presented along with a scrapbook, each reflecting and mutually supporting the other (see chap. 8).

Preserving Your Stories

Once your stories are written and arranged, you must address the form in which they will be preserved. The possibilities range from a pile of handwritten pages to a hand-sewn, hardcover book with a dust jacket. Which you choose will depend on your intended audience, your preferences, and your pocketbook.

Because of the digital revolution, it is now possible to put your own writing into a book format rivaling anything you find in a bookstore, without ever involving a traditional publisher. The single biggest change is that printers can now make a profit on small print runs, whereas in the past books had to be printed in the thousands to be affordable.

The second biggest change is that the specialists in the publishing process—editors, book designers, printers, marketers, distributors—who used to be controlled entirely by a publisher, are now available to individuals as freelancers. They cost money, of course, but they offer themselves to individuals and are great resources for information and execution.

A third change is that there are now professionals—generically called book manufacturers or author services providers—who are willing to undertake all or part of the process of seeing your writing from manuscript form to final product as a book. And there are publishing consultants who will do none of the physical work themselves, but will work out a publishing plan for you and offer recommendations for hiring out the specific services required. And, as I will discuss below, there are now a host of online and digital self-publishing companies that will allow you to do everything from home on your computer.

But self-published books can be quite expensive, so let's start more modestly. You need to ask yourself three questions about your collection:

How many copies do I need?

How do I want it to look?

How much am I willing to spend?

The answer to the first question establishes the quantity and may itself determine most of the subsequent choices. If you are going to produce only a handful of copies (say less than twenty-five), then you may want to do all the production work yourself. If you want hundreds of copies, you will almost certainly want help. And if you think you are going to sell what you have written (not a goal that I encourage), you are entering a different world altogether.

The answer to the second question (how do I want it to look?) will also be determinative. If you are happy with a text that looks like a project you would turn in at school or the office, then you can easily produce many copies of a story collection with modest effort and relatively little cost.

If you want the text to look like a book, however, then you will have to move from a word-processing program and photocopier to a text-design program and a professional printer. Some people can use a layout software program themselves if they have access to one on a computer, but most will need to hire a book designer to turn a file produced by a word-processing program into a file that can be printed to produce a book. This will require many decisions about gutters, margins, fonts, page number placements, word and line breaks, widowed lines, blank pages, signatures, photo placements, and on and on. If you don't know what some of those terms refer to, then you see the problem of doing it yourself.

The second question also requires you to consider issues like quality of paper, binding, and covers. Again, paper qualities and styles can range from generic white of the usual weight to parchment with ragged edges. And binding options start with paperclips and staples and work up to hand-sewn books with a ribbon bookmark. Covers range from cardstock to linen-covered boards. And a book designer can also create a dust jacket, should you decide to go the whole nine yards.

It is the third question (how much am I willing to spend?) that really decides all. After you have answered it, you may well have to go back and change your answers to questions one and two. You can spend twenty dollars or twenty thousand reproducing your stories. As so often in life, you will have to weigh desires against resources.

Five Scenarios

There are too many variables to directly answer the question, what will it cost to print my stories? But here are five scenarios, each symbolized by a mode of travel, that will give you a general idea.

THE VOLKSWAGEN BUG

When I was a kid the cheapest car available was a Volkswagen Bug. I recommend this approach for someone who cares little about the aesthetic quality of the final product and is not intending to produce very many copies. In such cases consider the following:

A. Create, revise, and edit the text yourself, using whatever method you prefer (pen and paper or computer), so long as you end up with a printed text.
B. Have a competent friend proofread it. (Everyone knows somebody who threw away their chance at riches by being an English major in college.) Make corrections.
C. Take it to the nearest copy or rapid-print store and have them help you pick out the cover material (probably cardstock) and form of binding (from staples to comb binding to thermal binding).

This is the fastest and least expensive way to produce your stories. It also results in the least satisfying product from an aesthetic point of view. It will cost a few hundred dollars at most.

THE CHEVY

If you want the final product to look like a book, but want to control costs, consider the following:

A. Create the text.
B. Hire a professional freelance editor to edit it.
C. Hire a book designer to layout the text in a design program and create a cover design (whether for a paper or hard cover). You can find local editors and designers on the internet.

194

D. Contact a few print companies *that specialize in books* and get multiple bids on printing and binding your book, in either paperback or hardcover.

If you hire the right people, this process will get you a book at moderate cost and with moderate effort that can look as good as any book in a bookstore. You should expect to pay a few hundred dollars for an editor, a few thousand dollars for a book designer, and a few thousand more for the printing, depending on numbers and production choices. If you want dozens or hundreds of copies of a good, book-quality version of your stories, expect to pay seven to ten thousand dollars and beyond.

The Cadillac

Just as you can hire someone to write your stories for you (see "personal historians" in chap. 8), you can also hire someone to take care of all of the steps of publishing your stories once they are written down. In this case you can do the following:

A. Create the text.
B. Find either a book manufacturer who specializes in self-publishing or a self-publishing book consultant (or author services company) and dump the project in their lap.
C. Make decisions on issues from paper to binding to cover as you are prompted, leaving them to execute your decisions.

This is the most expensive approach, but also the one that combines the least effort with a high-quality final product. Expect to pay ten to twenty thousand dollars, depending on how many books you finally order, understanding that the first fifty are by far the most expensive.

The Hybrid

You can also do a combination of the above in order to balance quality against costs:

A. Create the text.
B. Edit the manuscript yourself or with a friend.

C. Lay the text out in a garden-variety design program (perhaps again with the help of a friend).

D. Design a simple cover yourself.

E. Take your self-produced, digital file to a book printer to get bids on printing and binding.

This *may* produce a decent-looking book at an affordable price. Or it may look like what it is, a halfway effort by an amateur with a little professional help at the end. Expect the cost to be somewhere between that for the Volkswagen and the Chevy.

THE COMMERCIAL JET (ONLINE SELF-PUBLISHING AND PRINT ON DEMAND)

Another option to consider is the new world of self-publishing (more accurately, self-printing) offered by an ever-expanding host of online companies. They are the high-tech descendents of what used to be called "vanity presses," but they are revolutionizing the way books are being made and distributed.

The crucial elements for amateur writers are the relatively low cost of setting up digital files for a book and the ability to order books at reasonable per-copy prices in *small quantities* whenever they are needed. The latter is called "print on demand" (POD) and it is extremely attractive for those with *some* computer savvy (or a talented nephew) and at most a couple thousand dollars to spend.

Essentially, these companies offer a menu of services from which you choose. They are not publishers in the traditional sense in that they do not care anything about the quality of writing or whether it will sell. You, not a prospective book buyer, are their customer. They sell services to authors and they are happy to sell you more than you really need.

Typically, self-publishing services offer preexisting formats into which you pour your digitalized content. Most give you lots of boxes to fill in that will translate into titles, chapters, back-cover matter, and the like. They often will design a cover for you, or allow you to design a cover using their program, or allow you to submit your own separately produced cover design—all for a fee.

A big word of warning: the cost of pursuing online self-publishing can start small and get big very fast if you get carried away (that is, they will sell you a Volkswagen Bug, but they'd prefer to sell you a Cadillac). I call this approach *The Commercial Jet* because it can be relatively inexpensive if you fly in crowded coach class with no frills (typically less than five hundred dollars for set-up and four to six dollars per copy ordered), or wildly expensive if you get delusions of Nobel Prizes and decide to fly luxury class with cloth covers, dust jackets, distribution, marketing, and other add-ons. Be sure to include costs such as shipping in your calculations, which can vary greatly from company to company.

Stick as much as possible with the basic package each company offers, and resist add-ons and dreams of appearing with your book on *Oprah*. (The show has ended anyway.) Don't be seduced by ISBNs and marketing campaigns unless they are free. You are writing for a small group of people you care about. It's very, very unlikely that someone who doesn't know you is going to pay to read your stories, no matter how excellently written.

One advantage of this approach is the ease of making more copies. Once everything is set up, a simple request will generate more books. Do a lot of research before choosing a company (search "self-publishing" and "print on demand" on the internet to get started). Some are much more user-friendly than others. And some are more predatory (beware of bait-and-switch tactics). This approach can let you take advantage of the latest technology and publishing innovations, but it also limits you to dealing with people only online or by phone. It works fine for many, but there are also horror stories. Read any contract offered very carefully and stay realistic.

Sharing Your Stories with Others

An Audience List

The whole point of spiritual legacy work is to be of help to someone else. You can't do that without sharing your work with others. But that leaves open the questions of who, when, and how. Just as you are in control of what you write and what stories you tell, so also are you in control of when to share your legacy and with whom.

At one extreme, you may choose to keep what you have written to yourself during your own lifetime, allowing it to be discovered after your death. You can even provide a cover letter of sorts explaining why you have done this. Legacies keep. They do not become stale or outdated, as anyone knows who has discovered forgotten letters or journals or diaries of people long passed. So your legacy will keep until after you are gone if you so choose.

Most of us, however, will want to bless someone right now. For this approach, I suggest creating an *audience list*. This is something you can do at the time you are first making a story or character or values list, so that you have particular persons and faces in mind as you write. But if you did not do it during your writing process, do so now. Who, specifically, are the people you most want to benefit from the spiritual will you have written or the stories you have told? Some on that list may not yet be alive. Your legacy awaits their arrival.

Then add people who mean something to you even if they are not the primary beneficiaries. Who would take pleasure in your stories or your spiritual will? Consider adding people who are actual characters in some of the stories, even if you are not particularly close to them (perhaps a teacher or a former neighbor).

A Party

After you have done all of the above, have a party!

Invite most of the people on your list, adding anyone else who strikes your fancy or is good at partying. Have enough copies of your work for each person there. Read a story or two or selected passages. Or read your spiritual will. Tell everyone how much you care about them and how much fun you had writing these stories for them. Encourage them to write their own stories. Bless them. Feel like an author. Love your book. Be proud of yourself. Eat lots of food.

Not everyone can come to the party. For those far away, send the book or the spiritual will, with a letter saying what you feel about them and why you are sending your completed project. You don't need to say a lot—the work you are sending will speak for itself.

And remember, you are in control. You do not have to share everything you write as part of your spiritual legacy. Share what will be of help now. Keep the rest in your drawer until it is needed.

Are You Done Yet?

Are you done yet? God only knows. Some people will write a two-paragraph spiritual will and feel they have done what they need to do. And perhaps they have. I would be more than happy to have such a thing from my father or mother, or from any one of my grandparents, or from my great friend Jon, who died much too soon. If that were all that I had, I would consider it a blessing.

Others will collect and distribute their stories even as they are writing more. If the first book party was fun, why not have another? None of us have a shortage of stories from our pasts. And we all are living amid new stories every additional day of our lives. Spiritual wills, in fact, ought to be updated from time to time, because God and life do not leave you in the same place for long.

If spiritual legacy work has proved enjoyable and meaningful, there is no reason not to continue it to the end of your days.

Conclusion

There seems no way but the way of candor and curiosity to be remembered well by the people I care about. Some cold evening in their middle age, perhaps a grandchild or two will sit by the fire and read something I've written. In this way, the way of words and imagination, we'll cross time and space together.

John Burns

Airline passengers strolling down concourse A at Chicago's Midway Airport, named after the epic World War II sea and air battle, pass a monument inscribed with the following words from a Marine private who fought in the Pacific: "For all the guys that never returned, for all the men that gave that last effort and could not get back to be as fortunate as I, I will tell the kids about what you did and why." An old man now, Edgar R. Fox volunteers at elementary schools to tell these stories and keep this promise. It is a pure form of spiritual legacy work.

You have a promise to keep as well, whether you spoke it out loud or not. It is the promise the psalmist felt the pull of when declaring (Ps. 145:4, my translation),

> One generation shall praise Your works to another,
> And shall declare Your mighty deeds.

You are responsible to testify to the work of God in your life, to the events and people who have shaped you, to the values you hold most dear, to the things you have witnessed and from which you have learned. In short, you have a promise to keep to those you love—both now and in the future. You must pass on the hard-won wisdom that is interwoven in the experiences of your life.

I speak unapologetically about promises and responsibility, but it is equally right to emphasize again how much pleasure and encouragement are in store for you when you tell your stories. You will discover many things you did not know you knew. You will see how rich and meaningful and blessed your life has been to this point, and it will give you hope for the future.

You may discover what Frederick Buechner discovered as he looked back over his life.

There is no event so commonplace but that God is present within it, always hiddenly, always leaving you room to recognize him or not to recognize him, but all the more fascinatingly because of that, all the more compellingly and hauntingly. . . . Listen to your life. See it for the fathomless mystery that it is. In the boredom and pain of it no less than in the excitement and gladness: touch, taste, smell your way to the holy and hidden heart of it, because in the last analysis all moments are key moments, and life itself is grace.

Appendix A

Spiritual Legacy Questions

A lot of spiritual legacy work arises from questions posed about one's life. Here is a sampling. They are meant for reflection and writing. They can provide raw material for a spiritual will or, if you tie your answers to stories from your life, a story legacy.

What Do You Want Your Legacy to Be?

On September 11, 2001, many people made last calls from airplanes and burning offices to those they loved. If you had to make that call, what would you want to say, and to whom?

What is a good or successful life? What characteristics describe such a life?

Envision a great-grandchild that you will never meet who needs to know about you. What do you want him or her to know? About you? About life?

What do you think your lasting legacy would be if you died tomorrow? Are you content with that legacy? Why or why not?

What are your core values, and how are those core values seen in the way you try to live your life?

What would you hope is said about you at your funeral?

What are some things you feel passionate about? Why?

What are three lessons life has taught you? What are the stories behind each?

What are five significant things you believe to be true? What life experiences taught you each of them?

What have you done that you hope has made the world a slightly better place?

What did you once believe was important that you have changed your mind about? What caused the change?

What have you learned is important that you once paid little attention to? What caused the change?

What is a way in which the world is better than when you were growing up? Worse? Different?

How do you see God differently now than you once did? What caused the change?

Have you or someone you know ever done the right thing under difficult circumstances (moral courage)? Tell about it. Do the same for other virtues.

Who, specifically, would you like to benefit from your spiritual legacy?

What Have Been the Legacies of Others to You?

Whose spiritual legacy has benefitted you? What did you learn? Through what circumstances?

Who in your extended family has played an important part in shaping you? Which teacher, friend, person of faith, or coworker?

What character from history, literature, the Bible (or other sacred writings) has meant a lot to you? Why?

What did someone do for you that changed how you thought or felt about life? About yourself? About God?

What and who have been sources of hope for you in your life? For whom would you like to be a source of hope? How could you be so?

What would you like to say to someone from your past who is now dead?

What writer, artist, thinker, or leader has provided a spiritual legacy for you? What form did it take? What did you learn?

Appendix B

Values, Virtues, and Valuables

Sometimes in preserving a spiritual legacy we start with the values and abstractions and find the stories from our life to convey them. Other times we start with the stories that mean most to us and discover the spiritual truths within them that we want to pass on. When using the first approach to identify what you value, it can be helpful to be reminded of the possibilities.

The following is a partial list of values and virtues. A value is an abstraction, whereas a virtue is a value in action. Thinking about either can produce material for reflection and writing. Sometimes stating a core conviction or value requires more than a single word, so a list of sample assertions that suggest core convictions is also included as a prompt for your own.

Again, generating this kind of material can be helpful either for a spiritual will or for birthing stories.

Values and Virtues

Courage, honesty, love, integrity, prudence/wisdom, hope, faith, humor/wit, selflessness, generosity, gentleness, grace, sacrifice, hard work, dependability, forgiveness, tolerance, happiness, joy, endurance, sharing, community, diligence, friendship, dignity, frugality, piety, truth/truthfulness/truth-telling, peace, intelligence, justice, mercy, righteousness, patience, strength, respect, confidence, beauty, goodness, caring, purity, compassion/sympathy, consideration, courtesy/politeness, contentment, cooperation, creativity, determination, discernment, enthusiasm, excellence, loyalty, flexibility, calmness, helpfulness, honor, idealism, kindness, moderation, modesty, perseverance, holiness, prayerfulness, reliability, decisiveness, resoluteness, responsibility, reverence, discipline, sincerity, tact, trusting, trustworthiness, understanding, learning.

Others:_____

Ideas or Convictions

Success without love is failure. Truth is more important than _____.
Hard work trumps raw intelligence. Meaning is more important than
money—but harder to find. Failure is the foundation of success. "Freedom is just another word for nothing left to lose" (Janis Joplin).

Value-Laden Memories

Events that taught life lessons. Wisdom passed on from someone wise.
Key people who shaped me—how and when and where. First and last
experiences. Best and worst experiences. Turning points in life. Personal
successes and failures. Things you are proud of and things you wished
you had done differently. Happiest and most difficult periods of life.

Appendix C

Generating Topics

What to Write About

The best source of topics is your everyday life experience, past and present, *and* how you feel and think about it. There are endless ways of categorizing these experiences that can be helpful in prompting ideas for writing. The following are some examples of categories and a sampling of specific topics within a category. There is often overlap between categories.

Family: Portrayals of relatives—parents, siblings, grandparents, extended family. Family interactions and dynamics—good, bad, humorous, enlightening. Impact of a family member on you—in the past, over the years, how they shaped you, and the like. Family tales, legends, rumors, and favorite stories. Family traditions, holidays, crises, triumphs, celebrations, and vacations. Black sheep and princesses.

Neighborhood: Places you lived—both physical and emotional descriptions. Interesting neighbors. Lives of neighborhood children—their forms of play, their relationship dynamics. Socioeconomic or cultural/class insights gained from experience in suburban, rural, and urban communities.

School: Classmates, favorite or feared teachers, educational practices (good and bad), playground experiences, peer pressures, successes and failures and embarrassments, what was taught, school lunches, sports, social activities, buddies and bullies.

Childhood: Early memories, fears and pleasures, nature of play, adventures, how you thought about the world/life/faith/people/family, pets, favorite objects and activities, traumas, sickness, hopes for your future, special friends, how adults viewed children, popular culture of the time (books, films, songs, politics).

Spiritual and Religious Experience: nature of, denominational distinctives, Sunday school, teachers, pastors/priests/nuns/rabbis, rituals and traditions, spiritual experiences and development, views of God, favorite Bible stories and characters, memorable services, youth groups, pageants and performances, music, architecture, church politics, memorable fellow members, aspects appreciated and lamented, rebellions against, funerals and weddings, sermons, theological speculations, spiritual lessons, doubts and questionings, changing views and values.

Times of Transition: moving, marriage, divorce, job and career changes, births and deaths, losses and gains in relationships, education, graduations, health, changes in perspective or outlook, important books or artistic experiences, travel.

Work: variety of jobs, pros and cons, bosses and coworkers, disasters and disappointments, vocational successes, everyday routines, customers, lessons learned, funny experiences.

Friends: key friendships, adventures together, broken and healed relationships, impact, good and bad influences, shared interests, what was learned from.

Popular Culture: movies and movie stars, television programs, advertising, books, magazines, sports teams and individuals, clothing styles, styles generally in various areas, cars/trains/planes, public life and public places (parks, stadiums, streets), politics and politicians, food, public entertainment.

Everyday Life: common rituals and products, routine of an average day, domestic life (how a meal was made, washing clothes, mowing the lawn), favorite meals, how free time was spent, what people talked about, fads, racial and gender attitudes and experiences.

Everyday Objects: something on a shelf, a work of art, a photograph, an old letterman's jacket, a trophy, a stuffed fish, something inherited, a piece of furniture, a plant, a piece of equipment or tool, a machine.

Major Public Events: personal and public reaction to the Depression, Pearl Harbor, World War II and other wars, Sputnik, the Kennedy and King assassinations, the Beatles, the moon landing, the Challenger explosion, the fall of Communism, 9/11, a natural disaster.

Travel: places, occasion for (military, vacation, work), local customs, experiences, adventures and misadventures, fellow travelers, cultural distinctives, what was learned.

Firsts: childhood memory, Christmas, book read from, riding of bicycle or other accomplishment, communion, day of school or in the military or at work, kiss, broken heart, major disappointment or surprise, pet, sweetheart, thought of retirement.

Lasts: time with a friend or loved one, day of work or schooling or military service or living at home, payment (house, car, school loan), going-away party.

Mosts: embarrassing moment, exciting time of life, frightening experience, meaningful letter received, difficult thing had to do, significant spiritual experience.

Favorites: childhood or adult book, pet, teacher, pastor, relative, game, meal/dessert, movie star, politician, writer or artist, athlete/team, car, piece of clothing, memory of someone, photograph, object, memory of childhood or other period of life.

Appendix D

Additional Examples
of Spiritual Legacy Work

The following story, focusing on an event, was written by Vivien Stein-bach, a woman in her late sixties, and describes a famous and deadly Minnesota blizzard in 1940.

"Oh, Mama, do I have to wear my winter coat?"

"Yes, you do. It is the middle of November and you have to wear your winter coat."

I trudged off to school with my sister. The coat was hot, it itched, and I still did not want to wear it. But wear it I did. Charlotte would "tell" if I didn't. The walk home from school was the same—hot and itchy.

In spite of Mom's predictions, it had been another beautiful late fall day. The leaves covered the ground in the grove of black walnut trees close to the house. The five hundred chickens that roamed and scratched in the grove were boycotting the small chicken shed in favor of roosting in the trees. After the usual arguments and peckings over the choicest seats, the grove settled down for the night.

The next morning dawned cloudy, but very warm for early November. Late in the day a light rain began to fall. The temperature dropped just a little, and as many chickens as could

211

crowded into the chicken shed. The rest of them, about four hundred, found spots on the low branches of the trees, tucked their heads under their wings, and proceeded to wait out the rain. By evening the rain was heavy and the thermometer kept dropping.

Any time during the night when I woke, all I could hear was the sleet hitting the windows and the wind howling around the corners of the house. By morning the snow was heavy and deep and continuous. Dad packed Charlotte, my sister, and John, my brother, into the car for the rare treat of being driven to school. It was decided that I should stay at home. He was only able to drive a short distance before the fierceness of the storm convinced him to turn around and come home.

Now a huge concern was the fate of the chickens in the grove. The ones in the shed were fine, but very cold. The family bundled up to go outside—Mom, Dad, John, Charlotte, and me. Biggest sister June stayed in the house with baby brother Milton. We walked to the grove. Entombed in place by the ice formed by the rain and sleet were branches full of mounds of chickens. They looked like rows of miniature igloos.

Using ladders, Dad and John reached out under the mounds, grabbed a chicken leg or two and handed the bird down to Mom or Charlotte. With each hand carrying three or four chickens, they all plowed their way through the blinding and drifting snow to the barn. Now it was my turn to do my part. My job as a seven-year-old was to roll back a huge barn door to let them in and close it fast behind them. The four of them put the birds down on any spot of bare floor in the barn. (Being in the barn would allow the chickens to thaw out with the heat from the other animals.) Then I opened the door to let them go out for the next load, shut it quickly to keep the snow and wind out of the barn, and watch carefully for them to come back with hands full of chickens.

The storm continued to rage on. Each trip to the barn meant plowing a new path through deepening snow. The previous path had been completely obliterated by the drifting snow. Finally all the chickens were rescued. The cows and horses in the barn got used to the noise of five hundred murmuring chickens as they began to thaw out and find out that their legs would support them. (I am not sure that the other animals got used to the aroma of wet chicken feathers.)

The chicken carriers and the door opener trudged to the house for dry, warm clothes and bowls of hot homemade soup (probably chicken) and fresh bread. We stayed inside all day and listened to the storm rage.

By the next morning the storm had abated, but it was bitter cold. Huge snowdrifts were everywhere. In the barn were five hundred chickens that had recovered sufficiently to be quite a nuisance to the cows and horses. It was quite another process to get them into crates and get them to the big chicken house for the winter. But the thought that our egg-laying, grocery-money-producing chickens had survived made it all worthwhile. All but about a half dozen of the chickens survived. Some of the survivors wore the scars of battle in their combs and wattles, but they survived.

The snow plows came in a day or so—huge rotary snow plows that chewed up big machine-fuls of snow and then blew it out the side of the machine in a huge arc over the power lines and half a block into the fields. Life returned to normal routines of chores and school. We had lived through the Armistice Day Blizzard.

The following narrative poem, titled "By Feel," is by Elise Toedt, a woman in her early twenties. It focuses on a character.

Grandpa calls this time of year the "summer doldrums"

He is particularly down today,
the eye doctor having declared at his check-up
there is nothing more to be done for him:
he will soon be blind.

when the hollyhocks lean on each other for support in the
heat

For now, his right eye (with glasses)
is still good, but not peripherally.
He cannot read anymore.

213

and the petunias close their arthritic fists and shrivel up to
   die.

I have many memories of him in his armchair
at midnight: a book in one hand,
a magnifying glass in the other.

The grass like thin hair, brown and broken—

He picks the beans by feel now
and pushes stakes in the middle of his plants
so he knows where to water.

I think we will all be happy for the rain.

The following story is told by Dr. Steve Dagirmanjian, a man in his
sixties, and includes both storytelling and reflection. It focuses on an
event, a character, and a value and is titled, "Mississippi Bob." (The
following is excerpted from an unpublished 2006 article, "Ordinary
Kindness.")

Mississippi Bob always scared me. Several other boys in our
elementary school in an old New England mill town were more
physically imposing. But something about Bob broadcast "Pro-
ceed with caution." Maybe it was his dark, hooded eyebrows or
his slouching shuffle of a walk. Or maybe it was the fact that
on his first day at school he beat the snot out of the bully who
teased him at recess.

Bob moved into town from Mississippi to live with his grandmother following his parents' divorce and didn't know a soul in
the school. He kept to himself and not much was known about
him. So, naturally, a mystique grew up around him. Rumor
had it that he smoked cigarettes, and that he had a girlfriend
in junior high school. Before long he came to be regarded as
something of a cross between John Dillinger and Sonny Liston.
Not that he ever robbed people. We simply thought of him as
being tough and bad.

One morning walking to school, I saw him leaning against a
tree smoking a cigarette. Whatever feeble attempt I made to hide

214

my incredulity and fascination failed miserably. Mississippi Bob glared at me and snapped, "What are you looking at, moron?" I tucked my chin in my chest and scuttled along without a word while thinking to myself, "Point taken, Mr. Mississippi Bob, sir."

Since Bob and I shared no classes (we weren't even in the same grade) and didn't exactly travel in the same circles, we were no more than recognizable faces to each other. Truth is, he probably didn't even know my name, but I knew his the same way people know someone like Mike Tyson.

Later that year on a warm, early spring day, I was heading to my grandparents' home after school. This involved walking down the main street in town, by the hardware store, Mencow's Men's Shop, and Flagg's Pharmacy with its soda fountain. As was my habit, I turned into an alley between stores before a central intersection in order to shortcut the corner for myself. Ten feet into the alley two older boys whom I didn't know entered from the other end. As I approached them, they put their hands on their hips and set their legs apart, blocking my way.

"How much money do you have?" the shorter of the two demanded.

"None," I lied.

"Let me see," the speaker said as he stepped toward me and his buddy started to circle around me.

"No," I said, and they both began pushing me and backing me up against the alley wall. As they pressed their assault further, jabbing my chest and arms, and groping insistently at my pockets, a slight figure turned into the alley. It was Mississippi Bob.

For me this was like having Billy the Kid show up while I was being robbed by Jesse James. I had no idea what to expect. Given my reflexive fear of Bob, my emotions quickly accelerated toward panic.

The juvenile muggers barely took notice of Bob's progress through the alley while they were relishing their cat-with-mouse torment of me.

Their assault was interrupted when I heard Mississippi Bob ask, "What's going on?"

"None of your *@#*^#ing business," the mouthy one yapped at him.

"Well, it's my business, now."

This was the last thing the boys or I expected to hear. Startled, they stopped with me and turned to face Bob. Bob looked directly at me and pointed his index finger between my eyes. In my state I had to remind myself that it was only his finger—he couldn't shoot me with it. As a whirlwind of thoughts swirled through my head, I failed to anticipate what Bob said to me next. "You, get out of here!"

Dumbfounded at first, it took seconds that seemed like minutes to get my legs moving. I could hear words exchanged as I fled, but I was beyond comprehending what was being said. The next thing I knew, I was at my grandparents' house.

Several days passed before I saw Mississippi Bob again. Although my fear of Bob was now mixed with other feelings, I remained wary of him, so I looked to him for some sign of recognition or acknowledgement. He maintained his usual menacing glare that I took to mean, "Don't be bothering me, moron." I never thanked Bob for saving me that day.

Despite my failure to acknowledge what he had done for me, Bob's selfless act of courage and kindness had moved me deeply. More than his saving me from a beating or a mugging, I was struck that someone who did not even know my name thought me important enough to put himself in harm's way to help. Prior to this, in my mind's view, such acts were only to be expected from family members. Instead, I now saw myself connected to others in a way I had never before imaged. I felt more relevant to more people because Bob took the time to make my business his. His kindness told me that I mattered.

The following was written by Bruce Wiebe, a man in his late fifties. He wrote it for and read it at his father's funeral. He titles it "Daddy." Note how a description largely limited to external behavior can reveal a great deal about inner values and character.

I saw him working every day, and I worked beside him for thirty years. He shoveled faster than anyone I knew, and other farmers and his hired men talked about the swiftness and sureness of his hands on a shovel. How he could lay in straight pipe along ditches like a mason with his hair on fire, slicing open the ditch bank by each row, patting the bottom of the incision to firm it, dropping in the pipe, pressing with his foot to even the pipe lip with the water in the ditch he'd just pulled with the tractor. Then quickly pack the soil over the pipe, two quick pats, and a nimble step to the next row.

He'd do twenty acres of ditch in an hour. Before setting the pipe, he threw them from the back of the flatbed as I drove along. Our first pipe were heavy, rough segments of iron not meant for sailing accurately anywhere, but his forearms went at them like a dealer flipping blackjack cards, spiraling them into every other row while riding the slowly rolling truck.

I liked to see him tune-up a new shovel handle with water over days, and his true-temper shovel blades were always lighter, slicier things than the crude ones bought new at the hardware store. It took years to grind them just right by constant use in sand and the heavy and hard dirt that he never let dry on them, dipping them in the ditchwater to clean when he was finished.

Daddy knew steel and welding and nuts and bolts and always kept a miniature crescent wrench in a pocket for adjusting carburetors and restoring diesel lines after I'd run out of fuel in the middle of the field. On a Cat, he pulled ruler-straight furrows in a cloud of dust without a mask, goggles, or complaints, 100 degree air running over the manifold into his face.

He was indifferent to pain and sickness. He'd pull over, open the pickup door, throw up, and continue on. Once after such a display he said, "You have to keep going."

Cuts would show up on the back of his forearms, his hands, and as blood dripped he tightened the bolt on a cultivator shovel one yank more. Thirsty, he'd drop out of the pickup to the valve pouring out pump water and, in push-up position, drink the bubbling clear water.

If Paul wasn't the elements, I'm a toadstool. He was Adam, what a man was in this world before computers, air conditioning, drip irrigation and health insurance improved his working environment. He was of the water, the earth, the air, and the fire. He stood in valley heat dripping sweat into the ground. And out of the earth came crops and weeds, potatoes and gophers. He sliced, pulled, and burned those weeds with a propane rig and set dachshunds and his shovel's edge loose on the yellow-toothed-ugly rodents when they wormed into alfalfa field banks and drained or delayed the irrigation water into sunken road shoulders.

I love to think of him at work. I love that he was my Dad. And as his flesh inhabited this planet and I think of his working, I also think of him on his knees every morning digging other furrows, before daylight, praying to his Heavenly Father. Two weeks ago I told him how I loved that memory. He said, "I didn't do it because I wanted to be a good boy. I did it because I was desperate and knew there was nothing else to do."

Daddy, I love you.

Resources

The following are some of the many helpful books and websites for life writing. Search key words on the sites of online booksellers and you will find many other helpful books. And you're invited to visit my personal website at www.wordtaylor.com.

Legacy Work in General

Celebrations of Life. See www.celebrationsoflife.net.
Soleil Lifestory Network. Website at www.turningmemories.com.

Writing a Spiritual-Ethical Will

Barry Baines. *Ethical Wills: Putting Your Values on Paper*. 2nd ed. Cambridge, MA: Da Capo Press, 2006. Also see his website at www .ethicalwill.com.
Rachael Freed. *Women's Lives, Women's Legacies: Passing Your Beliefs and Blessings to Future Generations*. Minneapolis: Fairview Press, 2003. Also see her website at www.life-legacies.com.
Jack Reimer. *So That Your Values Live On: Ethical Wills and How to Prepare Them*. Woodstock, VT: Jewish Lights Publishing, 1994.

How to Write Memoirs and Life Stories

Lois Daniel. *How to Write Your Own Life Story: The Classic Guide for the Non-Professional Writer.* 4th ed. Chicago: Chicago Review Press, 1997.

Denis Ledoux. *Turning Memories Into Memoirs: A Handbook for Writing Lifestories.* Lisbon Falls, ME: Soleil Press, 2005.

Nan Phifer. *Memoirs of the Soul: Writing Your Spiritual Autobiography.* Cincinnati, OH: Walking Stick Press, 2001.

Dan Wakefield. *The Story of Your Life: Writing a Spiritual Autobiography.* Boston: Beacon Press, 1990.

William Zinsser. *Writing About Your Life: A Journey into the Past.* Cambridge, MA: Da Capo Press, 2005.

Discussions of Memoir and Life Writing

John Paul Eakins. *How Our Lives Become Stories: Making Selves.* Ithaca, NY: Cornell University Press, 1999.

Patricia Hampl and Elaine Tyler May. *Tell Me True: Memoir, History, and Writing a Life.* Wadena, MN: Borealis Books, 2009.

Roger C. Schank. *Tell Me a Story: Narrative and Intelligence.* Evanston, IL: Northwestern University Press, 1990.

William Zinsser, ed. *Inventing the Truth: The Art and Craft of Memoir.* Boston: Houghton Mifflin, 1998.

Aids for Life Writing

Ian Harrison. *Where Were You When? 180 Unforgettable Moments in Living History.* New York: Reader's Digest, 2008.

Robert Joyce, ed. *Astonishing Century.* Hawthorne House Books, 1999. List of specific historical, political, media, and popular culture events for each year from 1900 to 1999. (Out of print)

Mary O'Brien Tyrrell. *Memoirs, Inc.* Website: www.memoirsinc.com. A professional memoir service that interviews and writes the memoirs of seniors.

Website for the Association of Personal Historians: www.personal historians.org.

Website for Editorial Freelancers Association (professional freelance editors, writers, desktop publishers, and the like): www.the-efa.org.

My Other Books Related to Life Writing

Letters to My Children: A Father Passes on His Values. St. Paul, MN: Bog Walk Press, 1989.

Tell Me a Story: The Life-Shaping Power of Our Stories. St. Paul, MN: Bog Walk Press, 1996.

In Search of Sacred Places: Looking for Wisdom on Celtic Holy Islands. St. Paul, MN: Bog Walk Press, 2005.

Examples of Well-Known Memoirs and Related Writings (there are hundreds)

Maya Angelou. *I Know Why the Caged Bird Sings*.

Augustine. *Confessions*.

Russell Baker. *Growing Up*.

Frederick Buechner. *The Sacred Journey; A Room Called Remember; Now and Then; Telling Secrets; The Eyes of the Heart*.

Annie Dillard. *Modern American Memoirs (ed.); Pilgrim at Tinker Creek; Holy the Firm; Teaching a Stone to Talk; For the Time Being*.

Izak Dinesen. *Out of Africa*.

Henry Louis Gates Jr. *Colored People*.

Patricia Hampl. *A Romantic Education; Virgin Time; The Florist's Daughter*

Margery Kempe. *The Book of Margery Kempe*.

C. S. Lewis. *Surprised by Joy*.

Nelson Mandela. *A Long Walk to Freedom*.

Nadezhda Mandelstam. *Hope Against Hope: A Memoir*.

Czeslaw Milosz. *Native Realm: A Search for Self-Definition*.

N. Scott Momaday. *The Names; The Way to Rainy Mountain*.

Anna Mary Moses. *Grandma Moses: My Life Story*.

Barbara Myerhoff. *Numbering Our Days*.

Rachel Naomi Remen. *My Grandfather's Blessings*.

Richard Rodriguez. *Hunger of Memory*.
Aleksandr Solzhenitsyn. *The Gulag Archipelago*.
Henry David Thoreau. *Walden*.
Eudora Welty. *One Writer's Beginnings*.
Elie Wiesel. *Night; Legends of Our Time*.

Notes

Introduction

xi **My story is important not because it is mine** Frederick Buechner, *Telling Secrets: A Memoir* (San Francisco: HarperOne, 1992), 30.

Chapter 1

1 **Dad Finds Work During the Great Depression—1934** Marilyn Boe, *The 17th Avenue Poems* (published by author, 1991).

10 **nothing has been learnt in here this afternoon** Athol Fugard, *Master Harold and the Boys* (New York: Penguin, 1982), 59.

12 **Wisdom is often ascribed** Roger C. Schank, *Tell Me a Story: Narrative and Intelligence* (Evanston, IL: Northwestern University Press, 1990), 14.

12 **Buckminster Fuller's knots** Hugh Kenner, *The Pound Era* (Berkeley: University of California Press, 1971), 145–46.

13 **We have large cemeteries** James Birren, Informal remarks made at the *International Reminiscence and Life Review Conference 2001*, Chicago, October 11, 2001.

19 **The medieval meaning of "solemn"** Thomas Howard, *Dove Descending: A Journey Into T. S. Eliot's Four Quartets* (San Francisco: Ignatius Press, 2006), 68.

Chapter 2

25 **the disposition of "moral" assets** Barry Baines, *Ethical Wills: Putting Your Values on Paper*, 2nd ed. (Cambridge, MA: Da Capo Press, 2006) 13.

25 **Women passing on wisdom** Rachael Freed, *Women's Lives, Women's Legacies: Passing Your Beliefs and Blessings to Future Generations* (Minneapolis: Fairview Press, 2003).

25 **Legal wills bequeath *valuables*** Baines, *Ethical Wills*, 14.

27 **What about the main thing in life** Alexander Solzhenitsyn, *The Gulag Archipelago*, vol. 1 (New York: Harper & Row, 1973), 591–92.

28 **a list of "hopes"** Lee Pitts, *People Who Live at the End of Dirt Roads* (Layton, UT: Gibbs Smith, 1995), 107–10.

30 **a grudge from the grave** Jack Reimer. *So That Your Values Live On: Ethical Wills and How to Prepare Them* (Woodstock, VT: Jewish Lights Publishing, 1994), xix.

35 **Distinction between "instructions" and "blessings"** Rachael Freed, *The Women's Legacies Workbook for the Busy Woman* (MinervaPress, 2005), 66.

36 **Who knows whether I shall be clear-minded** Reimer, *So That Your Values Live On*, 3.

Chapter 3

53 **tell their own story** Ignazio Silone, *Fontamara,* trans. Harvey Fergusson II (New York: Dell, 1961), 15.

66 **no man is an island** John Donne, "Meditation 17," from *Devotions Upon Emergent Occasions.*

Chapter 5

97 **master story** Michael Goldberg, *Jews and Christians: Getting our Stories Straight* (Nashville: Abingdon, 1985), 23.

Chapter 6

136 **I don't believe in a writer's kicking around people** Annie Dillard, "To Fashion a Text," in *Inventing the Truth*, ed. William Zinsser (Boston: Houghton Mifflin, 1998), 156.

Chapter 7

141 **I Tell My Mother Lies** Daniel Taylor, "I Tell My Mother Lies," first appeared in *Image: A Journal of the Arts and Religion*, no. 64 (Winter 2009–2010).

158 **an exhibitionist nor a masochist** Denis Ledoux, *Turning Memories into Memoirs: A Handbook for Writing Lifestories* (Lisbon Falls, ME: Soleil Press, 1993), 100.

158 **the dignity of movement of an iceberg** Ernest Hemingway, *The Hemingway Reader*, ed. Charles Poore (New York: Scribners, 1953), xvi.

160 **I have no grievances left** Dillard, *Inventing the Truth*, 155.

Chapter 9

187 **Choose people who will critique the work** Ledoux, *Turning Memories into Memoirs*, 70.

Made in the USA
Monee, IL
09 April 2021